Vintage
Volkswagen Beetle
Accessories

INCLUDES *Beetle • Karmann Ghia • Bus • Type 3*

CarTech®

Stephan Szantai

CarTech®, Inc.
6118 Main Street
North Branch, MN 55056
Phone: 651-277-1200 or 800-551-4754
Fax: 651-277-1203
www.cartechbooks.com

Edit by Bob Wilson
Layout by Connie DeFlorin

ISBN 978-1-61325-750-0
Item No. CT689

Library of Congress Cataloging-in-Publication Data Available

Written, edited, and designed in the U.S.A.
Printed in China
10 9 8 7 6 5 4 3 2 1

CarTech books may be purchased at a discounted rate in bulk for resale, events, corporate gifts, or educational purposes. Special editions may also be created to specification. For details, contact Special Sales at 6118 Main Street, North Branch, MN 55056 or by email at sales@cartechbooks.com.

PUBLISHER'S NOTE: In reporting history, the images required to tell the tale will vary greatly in quality, especially by modern photographic standards. While some images in this volume are not up to those digital standards, we have included them, as we feel they are an important element in telling the story.

DISTRIBUTION BY:

Europe
PGUK
63 Hatton Garden
London EC1N 8LE, England
Phone: 020 7061 1980 • Fax: 020 7242 3725
www.pguk.co.uk

Australia
Renniks Publications Ltd.
3/37-39 Green Street
Banksmeadow, NSW 2109, Australia
Phone: 2 9695 7055 • Fax: 2 9695 7355
www.renniks.com

Canada
Login Canada
300 Saulteaux Crescent
Winnipeg, MB, R3J 3T2 Canada
Phone: 800 665 1148 • Fax: 800 665 0103
www.lb.ca

TABLE OF CONTENTS

Acknowledgments 6

About the Author.. 6

Foreword By Keith Seume 7

Introduction... 8

Chapter 1: 1945–1967: Rising from the Rubble 9

Chapter 2: The Post-1967 Years: New Car, New Era 21

Chapter 3: Exterior Details: Dressed up and Ready to Go..............................34

Chapter 4: Interior Details: Get Inside and Get Comfortable 44

Chapter 5: Embracing Diversity: Accessories for the Entire VW Family 56

Chapter 6: Engine and Performance: Putting Some Muscle into It.................66

Chapter 7: Wheels: Rolling Down the Road in Style.......................................76

Chapter 8: Traveling: Happily Hitting the Street..88

Chapter 9: Old Speed: A Trend Rooted in Old European Auto Races............98

Chapter 10: California Look: When Drag Racing Meets the Street 109

Chapter 11: Resto Cal Look: Low and Loaded with Accessories 122

Chapter 12: A Notch Above: Detailed, Stylish, and Fully Accessorized 132

ACKNOWLEDGMENTS

The author wants to thank the following people: My wonderful wife, Tania, who is always by my side, always the trooper, and always ready to help with my written material; Georg Otto for giving me full access to his collection of vintage magazines; respected author/journalist Keith Seume for his support and for writing this book's foreword; Mike Walravens and Laurent "El Dub" Dubois (search cal-look.no/nostalgia) for their pictures and inexorable enthusiasm; the late Bill Mortimer for his vintage photos; Shin Mukai and Shin Watanabe for publishing *hotVWs* magazine, following in the footsteps of other talented journalists/enthusiasts since 1967; Jim Aust for allowing me to photograph his impressive collection of *Foreign Car Guides*; the great automotive journalists David Fetherston and Tony Thacker for their valuable advice; Blaine Braziel for the photos of his beautiful Formula Vee–equipped Beetle; the editors/contributors of the 20-plus Volkswagen magazines I have had the chance to work with; my fellow Der Kleiner Panzers VW club friends for their support; the folks whose cars appear in this book, often following long photo sessions.

Incidentally, any mention of ownership refers to the person in possession of the vehicle when the pictures were shot.

ABOUT THE AUTHOR

Born and raised in France from a German mother and a Hungarian father, Stephan Szantai has had a deep interest in automobiles for longer than he can remember. Regular childhood trips to Germany to visit an aunt who drove a 1971 Beetle sealed his fondness for air-cooled Volkswagens.

A fascination for car magazines led to Stephan's first article that was published in France's then-new *Super VW* magazine in 1987. Five years later, a business opportunity prompted him to move to Southern California, a region with a rich car culture. Some sporadic work for European publications followed, until freelance automotive journalism as a writer and photographer became his full-time occupation in 2000.

Stephan poses with his sunroof Bug. Visually, the car has not changed much since it was built in 1984. He and the 1957 belong to Der Kleiner Panzers, which is a prominent Southern Californian club founded in 1965 and is dedicated solely to high-performance air-cooled Volkswagens.

Fast-forward over two decades. Stephan's career has translated into books along with 2,500 articles printed in nearly 100 automotive magazines based in 17 countries. Old Volkswagens remain very much part of his life today thanks to both his involvement with the scene and the 2.3L 1957 Beetle he purchased in 1993.

FOREWORD

By Keith Seume
Automotive Journalist

On the surface, it makes no sense. The very process of adding accessories to a Volkswagen Bug goes against the whole ethos of the People's Car, which was to provide a basic means of transport designed solely to get the occupants from Point A to Point B with the minimum of fuss and at the least expense. Yet, human nature being what it is, it was only a matter of time before owners began stamping their own mark on Dr. Porsche's car for the masses. After all, who wanted to drive something that looked exactly the same as his or her neighbor's car?

Many early accessories were designed to make the Bug look, well, less Bug-like, such as extra body trim or fancy wheel embellishers. Inside, radios, reclining seat conversions, headrests, and, of all things, flower vases reflected all the comforts of home in an effort to make long journeys seem less tiring. Practical accessories, such as mudflaps and fly deflectors, helped keep the car clean, while racks and roof-mounted tents turned the Bug into a holiday home on wheels. By the end of the 1950s, there was hardly anything you couldn't buy for your Bug.

Of course, not every accessory was as whimsical as a flower vase or extra body trim. Many were purely practical in nature. Additional driving lamps helped owners see down the road at night when the original weak 6-volt headlights proved woefully inadequate in the depths of a harsh winter. Extension lamps, which could be plugged into the factory-fitted cigarette lighter (an accessory installed by Volkswagen from the earliest days), helped facilitate the changing of a punctured tire or fixing an engine problem by the roadside at night. Toolkits or emergency gas tanks that fitted into the spare wheel were also popular.

A vast industry grew rapidly around this hunger for add-ons and equally as rapidly went into decline as the cars became better equipped straight from the factory over the years. Then, in the 1980s, something strange happened. Enthusiasts began collecting these accessories, hunting down examples to fit their own classic Bugs or to simply sit in a display case in a man cave. Accessories began to change hands for ever-increasing sums of money, some costing a few dollars, others costing hundreds if not thousands in the case of engine conversion kits, such as those offered by Okrasa in Germany.

In the early 1990s, I bought a 1951 Split Window Beetle that had been lovingly and sympathetically restored by an enthusiast a few years earlier. Its appeal was the fact it had been fitted with one of these Okrasa engine conversions, which almost doubled the feeble 25-hp power output. I loved it, but the accessory bug had bitten.

Before long, I began collecting as many period-correct accessories as I could from fancy steering wheels to parcel nets and from driving lamps to license plate holders. I became obsessed, scouring swap meets for trinkets, swapping parts with others, and searching out the obscure. Accessories get you that way.

Stephan's book has helped fill a void that has existed for far too long, telling the story, spreading the gospel of how loving owners turned the basic Bug into a personal expression. Enjoy the read—who knows, perhaps it will inspire you to go treasure hunting!

Keith Seume
Cornwall, UK

A few years ago, Keith Seume owned this 1951 sedan that is a well-known Beetle within the vintage VW scene. Several accessories equipped the exterior, such as mudflaps, an exhaust tip, and a Belgian license plate topper. Behind the lid lurked a desirable Okrasa powerplant.

INTRODUCTION

Volkswagen trends have undoubtedly changed since the 1980s, when I drove a 1965 Bug and joined the growing bunch of young VW enthusiasts who shared the same interest. Living in Europe back then, I had the opportunity to attend a range of Volkswagen events. The local scene truly exploded around 1987 thanks to shows such as the first Bug Jam at Santa Pod Raceway, UK. I also visited the Bad Camberg VW vintage meet in Germany that year, and it left its mark on my memory as well. Looking at the photos that I took at the time, it is quite surprising to see how few vehicles—even the best restored models—sported period accessories.

With the above-mentioned 1965 Beetle, I joined a club called Wild VW & Buggy, which went on to organize the first major Volkswagen show in France in 1986, known as VW Connection. In 1987, the second VW Connection attracted a larger number of foreign visitors, including Ulf Kaijser, who drove his dark green 1956 Oval Window Beetle all the way from Sweden. His restored sedan stood out in a sea of bright and cheery vehicles with more than 40 vintage accessories and a 1200-cc motor equipped with a 1950s Judson supercharger. The car (shown in Chapter 3) was unlike anything I'd ever seen before. It later morphed into a monster affair after being renamed Super VW National with more than 2,700 air-cooled models by the early 1990s.

Over the decades, non-factory pastel hues and custom body modifications slowly fell by the wayside. Enthusiasts now prefer using subdued colors, often selected from original VW paint charts while keeping the outside appearance of their rides stock or near stock.

Full customs have become rarities, but it does not mean that Volkswagen buffs refuse to individualize their vehicles—far from it. Go to any present-day VW show, and it is apparent that most cars feature lowered suspension and aftermarket wheels. Custom alterations are a lot more subtle as well, from one-off machined components to uncluttered engine compartments.

Period-correct accessories have become another popular way to personalize the same air-cooled toys. Indeed, these add-ons have seeped through various segments of the scene. For instance, take the vintage crowd. It might appreciate an early 1950s Beetle equipped with uncommon side mirrors, extra fog lights, and rear fender skirts. Others prefer low-to-the-ground Volkswagens. So, how about a Type 3 Squareback (station wagon) featuring a roof rack, reclining seats, and a rare steering wheel?

Even fans of street-driven high-performance Volkswagens might search for desirable 1960s EMPI wheels or an early 1970s Gene Berg carburetor linkage. Some individuals also emulate Beetles that look as if they might have been rally racing in Europe during the 1950s courtesy of old carburetor kits, equally old gauges, etc. The possibilities are endless.

Based on the realization that vintage Volkswagen accessories captivate a wide audience, I began tinkering with the idea of writing a book about the subject a few years ago. Lack of time put its conception on the backburner until the 2020 pandemic hit. It reshaped the economy, the way of doing business, and many other aspects of our lives, including mine. Suddenly, that book seemed like an appealing Covid-19-era project, and I went to work.

True to the original outline, the following pages will hopefully entice the most hardcore VW buffs as well as folks with a wider range of car interests. Compiling the book proved to be both fascinating and daunting, considering the hundreds (or could it be thousands) of accessories offered for all sorts of air-cooled Volkswagens since World War II. In fact, I purposely decided to concentrate only on the 1945 to 1980 period, being so rich in products available, although the industry continued flourishing afterward. Hmmm . . . Maybe an idea for a sequel, eh?

CHAPTER 1

1945-1967:
RISING FROM THE RUBBLE

Henry Ford undoubtedly helped put America on the road with his Model T, which was released in 1908. However, owning a car remained a far-fetched dream for the average worker in the rest of the world, especially between World War I and World War II.

In Germany, Adolf Hitler (the country's chancellor since January 1933) had the grandiose vision of motorizing his fellow citizens with a small automobile. He knew precisely who to put in charge of the project: a talented Austrian-German automotive engineer by the name of Ferdinand Porsche.

Volkswagen Takes Over the World

In the fall of 1933, Porsche and Hitler met, and Hitler highlighted the bold features of the vehicle he envisioned. It had to carry four people and their luggage,

This brochure from 1953 reveals the array of products sold by the German company Happich: an exterior sun visor, reclining seat, lit Deutschland "D" bumper plate, pop-out window with smooth frame, etc.

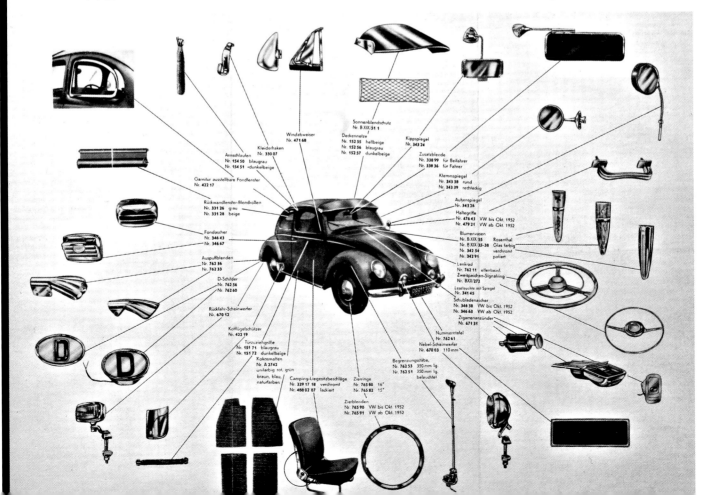

Only a handful of KdF-Wagens (the Beetle's World War II predecessor) are known to exist today. Photographed in Tokyo, Japan, this 1943 example belongs to Volkswagen collector Takashi Komori, who is the founder of Flat4, a purveyor of VW parts and accessories since 1976.

offer a fuel consumption of 7 liters per 100 km (about 33 mpg), and sustain a speed of 100 kph (62 mph) on the newly built Autobahn (freeway) network. Furthermore, the expected price tag was set at 990 Reichsmarks, which is an incredibly low figure when compared to a small and basic 995-cc Opel for instance, which cost 1,890 Reichsmarks that same year.

It took more than four years of grueling testing and development to finally bring forth this icon of the automobile world that is better known as the *Beetle* or *Bug* in the English language. On May 28, 1938, a crowd of more than 50,000 came to watch Hitler during a cornerstone ceremony in Northern Germany. It was organized on the site of the future factory designed to build the new little car.

Three models were displayed in front of the stage where Hitler pronounced his speech: a hardtop sedan, a sunroof sedan, and a convertible. The trio already looked remarkably close to the Beetles many of us came to love.

Although most people involved in the project called it *Volkswagen* (People's Car), Hitler insisted on giving the vehicle a different appellation: KdF-Wagen. The initialism KdF stands for *Kraft durch Freude* (Strength through Joy), which was the name of a state-operated leisure organization in Nazi Germany. Indeed, the dictator saw the car as a great propaganda tool.

The plant's site also gave birth to *Stadt des KdF-Wagens bei Fallersleben* (City of the KdF-Wagens at Fallersleben), which was a new town set around the village of Fallersleben built to house the factory's workers. Today, this thriving urban community of 125,000 residents is better known as Wolfsburg, where the VW factory plays a key role in the automotive industry.

Along Came the War

World history changed the fate of an automobile that many Germans had hoped to drive by the early 1940s. In September 1939, Hitler sent his troops to invade Poland, which was an event that led Great Britain and France to declare war on Germany. Soon, the new factory was used to support the country's military effort, mostly building all-terrain, rear-engined vehicles such as the Kübelwagen (Type 82) and the amphibious Schwimmwagen (Type 166).

By the mid-1940s, as the conflict drew to an end, the plant had produced about 50,000 Kübelwagens and close to 15,000 Schwimmwagens. Only a handful of KdF-Wagens rolled out of the assembly line from 1941 to 1944. The first, labeled either Type 92 (1941 until April 1943) or Type 82E (afterward), offered excellent off-road abilities due in part to all-terrain suspension components borrowed from the Kübelwagen. Another version, known as the Type 60, featured a lower ride height akin to most Split Window Bugs built after the war. Yet, the rarest of the rare remains the Type 87 equipped with four-wheel drive.

Production figures of these World War II Beetles remain a subject of contention, although automotive historians often suggest a total of 560 Type 92/82Es and 630 Type 60s—the latter were often driven by the Nazi elite. Incidentally, KdF-Wagens have become some of the most valuable collectible models in the VW scene with only a few dozen being documented today. A number of these treasures remained locked in Eastern European countries after the war in a part of the world closely watched by the Union of Soviet Socialist Republics (USSR).

The same factory that produced the KdF-Wagens during World War II also manufactured military vehicles, such as the amphibious Schwimmwagen. Both models used the same air-cooled flat-four motor.

During the decades that followed, many Westerners dreamed of bringing over these vehicles from the other side of the iron curtain, but only a handful of enthusiasts succeeded. The fall of the Berlin Wall in November 1989 and the subsequent political events made the situation much easier for collectors, who have since been able to unearth several of these mega-rare Beetles.

An Ailing Country

With many large industrial cities reduced to a heap of rubble, Germany faced an uphill battle after the end of World War II, starting with a food shortage that lasted until 1948. The heavily bombed production infrastructure required being rebuilt as well to put the country back on track. This included the battered factory making the KdF-Wagens.

Following the VW plant's liberation by U.S. troops in April 1945, Stadt des KdF-Wagens bei Fallersleben became Wolfsburg in May that year. The KdF-Wagen moniker soon disappeared as well, being replaced by Volkswagen.

In June, British military forces took over operation under the watchful eye of Major Ivan Hirst (1916–2000). His team confronted significant hurdles to relaunch manufacturing of the Beetle sedan. Post–World War II shortages (sheet metal and coal in particular) affected production as did the weather during the winter months. A cold spell forced Volkswagen to close the assembly lines from December 1946 until March 1947. As a result, the Wolfsburg factory built only 8,987 vehicles in 1947, which totaled about 1,000 fewer units than 1946.

Based on these premises, one might understand why the Bug was pretty much the antithesis of a luxury automobile during the 1940s, especially when considering that the first VWs produced did not land in civilian hands. The Allies took delivery of these workhorses, being shared by armed forces and government agencies from three countries: the United States, England, and France. Even the USSR got 20 of them before the beginning of the Cold War, according to an interview with Major Hirst.

At a time when Volkswagen struggled to obtain key components, such as glass, for the Beetle, the factory's executives didn't see fit to install chrome bumpers, shiny moldings, and other fancy frills—as you might have guessed.

By 1948, an increasing number of civilians finally had the opportunity to purchase the "People's Car," which

During the mid-to-late 1940s, the early Beetles were the antithesis of well-equipped automobiles, as demonstrated by Steve Beecher's stark 1947 sedan. It was one of 8,987 manufactured that year. Not a single speck of chrome adorns the body.

In 1949, Volkswagen introduced the Deluxe model featuring aluminum moldings and plenty of chrome. Customers could also purchase the entry-level Standard. For comparison, take a look at Larry Luhrsen's 1952 sunroof Deluxe and Jim Logudice's 1952 hardtop Standard.

Adolf Hitler had promised them more than a decade earlier. The Bug still remained stark by design, but this all changed when the automaker launched an improved version of its sedan in the middle of 1949: the Deluxe Beetle.

This model proves especially interesting in the context of this book, as it might be considered the first "accessorized" VW in a way. It was meant to appeal to German clients as well as potential foreign buyers when Volkswagen finally began exporting the Bug. This explains why Americans in particular often use the "Export" label to describe the Deluxe.

Compared to the stark Standard model that was still offered in Germany, the Deluxe/Export featured a number of upgrades, including body moldings (hood, sides, and running boards), additional chrome (bumpers, handles, headlight rings, hubcaps), a VW emblem on the hood, etc. A single sun visor and various ivory knobs adorned the cockpit, while the front seats slid on rails unlike the Standard Bugs, which had seats still affixed to the floor with wing nuts.

The German Miracle

By the time the 1950s came along, Germany was on its way to a stellar economic recovery. More folks could afford a Volkswagen, often choosing the better-equipped Deluxe/Export. With income slowly improving, citizens occasionally splurged on accessories.

A few entrepreneurs paved the way during the postwar years, offering practical gear, such as trailer hitches and the first radios. After all, when conceived in the

Volkswagen enthusiasts actively seek early issues of Germany's **Gute Fahrt,** *the world's oldest VW-related magazine, which is still published to this day. A Deluxe Bug graced the cover of the first issue, which was released in October 1950.*

This is the city of Bad Camberg, Germany, the home of one of the world's most famous vintage Volkswagen shows in 1987. At the time, few VW buffs had any interest in old, original accessories.

By the early 1950s, VW drivers could select from a wide array of accessories, including a VDO fuel gauge, Rohde & Schwartz radio, Petri steering wheel, small Westfalia trailer, etc.

Hazet offered toolboxes that fit smartly in the middle of the spare wheel.

1930s, the Beetle featured a dash designed to receive a clock or audio equipment to the right of the sole gauge. More companies jumped on the bandwagon by the end of the 1940s. By 1950, VW clients had access to a wide range of goodies.

To prove this point, look at the pages of a German magazine solely dedicated to Volkswagens: *Gute Fahrt*. The name can be translated in various ways, including "safe journey" or "good trip." The first issue hit the newsstands in October 1950, and it became an instant success.

Amazingly, the publication is still printed 70-plus years later, which is quite an accomplishment in the automotive world. However, it should be said that its content pertains first and foremost to new cars from the VW group (including Porsches, Audi, Škoda, and Seat). Not much air-cooled material trickles through the pages besides the odd article about the most prevalent vintage VW shows.

Color publications were expensive to print in the 1950s, hence *Gute Fahrt* made do with black-and-white pages. Ads often featured simple, restrained designs and a photo or two. Talented artists occasionally helped generate great advertisements, and some are pure delight.

Gute Fahrt's content showed the incredible diversity of the VW products already available. Full pages often mixed a variety of ads from steering wheels and tachometers to radios and locking steering columns. Even Westfalia (a company known worldwide for its Bus-based campers sold via VW dealers) promoted its small trailers.

Some merchandise could be purchased through the VW network, such as a round toolbox that fit in the center of the spare wheel, which is highly sought after by collectors today. The 1951 ad claims *Original Ersatzteile* ("Original Spare Parts") with no mention of the manufacturer, although it appears to be a model made by Hazet.

Other advertising firms linked to the VW name include Hella and Bosch, which were known for their headlights and horns, respectively. Their offerings mixed accessories (often chromed) and straight replacements for stock parts.

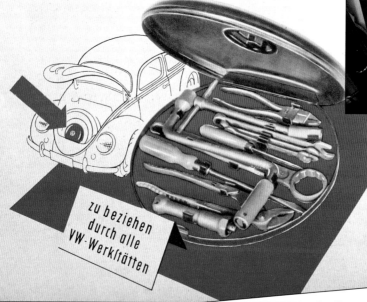
Customers could buy tool kits through local Volkswagen dealerships, being Original VW Ersatzteile ("Original VW Spare Parts"). This ad is dated July 1951.

There are countless ways to personalize a Volkswagen by combining accessories. When it comes to steering wheels, one may add a horn ring plus one of the dozens of vintage horn buttons available through the years. This picture is from Flat4's headquarters in Japan.

The early 1950s saw the advent of major players in the VW aftermarket, starting with Happich, which launched in 1924 and is still active today. It created an extensive line for both the exterior and the interior with such gems as pop-out side windows (with smooth frames) and seat recliners. Also in existence today, Kamei became another successful company with a range of accessories that put the emphasis on driving enjoyment.

Beetle owners could add more equipment to spruce up the cockpit—for example, in the shape of a handsome-looking Petri steering wheel. Want to enjoy the summer breeze? Although VW offered optional sunroofs made by Golde as early as 1950, a *Gute Fahrt* ad from 1954 shows a fairly similar version sold by Webasto, (the manufacturer also made a smaller offering a few years later for Karmann Ghia coupes). Occasionally, the pages of the magazine unveiled some rather unusual products in the vein of dual pedal assemblies for driving school Bugs (1952).

While Volkswagen marketed the Beetle with an optional sunroof as early as 1950, customers could also have one installed afterward in a hardtop sedan with a kit supplied by Webasto.

America's Love Affair

Until the mid-1950s, the bulk of the accessories were sold first and foremost in Germany. Another market soon offered exciting business opportunities: the United States. Volkswagen had mixed results promoting its vehicles in the United States until it established Volkswagen of America (VWoA) in 1955. Beetles in particular soon invaded the roads from New York to Los Angeles.

Americans already had a tradition of customizing and hot rodding automobiles by that time. Therefore, some companies eagerly came up with new products while others began selling them. To reach their customers, these firms relied on the press once again, starting in 1956 with a publication called *Foreign Car Guide* (*FCG*). It mostly revolved around non-domestic vehicles, as you might expect, but the subheading "Featuring Volkswagen" clearly stated the targeted readership.

Seeing double? This 1955 Oval Window Bug intended for driver education features dual controls, allowing the passenger to steer and operate the three pedals.

Small ads sprinkled the pages of 1950s Gute Fahrt *magazines, as exemplified by this June 1952 medley. Ten companies shared the space, promoting an extensive assortment of products, such as a pedal assembly for driving school Beetles.*

Offered in 1953, Fischer's "Schwenktank" (swivel tank) contained an extra 22 liters/5.8 gallons of gas. It mounted behind the Beetle's factory fuel tank. When the latter was nearly empty, one simply pivoted this aftermarket reservoir and then turned a lever to dump its contents in the stock tank. Voilá!

Starting in 1956, American VW fans could discover the latest accessory offerings courtesy of Foreign Car Guide, a small-format magazine with a strong emphasis on the VW brand.

Published in Ohio, *FCG* featured a small format (5.5x8 inches). Its circulation was somewhat sporadic between 1956 and 1959 with a little more than 20 issues hitting the newsstands. However, it became monthly in the early 1960s.

The paper and printing remained average at first, while all pages appeared in black and white as was still the tradition with the vast majority of magazines of the time. Quality later improved, and *FCG* even adopted a larger format in the late 1960s. However, by 1972, this staple of the VW scene was gone.

Other American automobile publications took an interest in the little Volkswagen as well, including *Sports Cars Illustrated*, which ran an article in July 1956 showing the high-performance potential of the flat-four engine.

Fisher Products began importing the "world's finest accessories for foreign and sports cars" during the 1950s. This ad dated October 1960 indicated the two main brands it promoted: Abarth and MotoMeter.

The piece in question listed some products available: Iskenderian camshafts, Judson superchargers (available for $159.50), Progressive Engine Products Company (PEPCO) superchargers ($199.50), and 80-mm pistons leading to a displacement of 1284 cc instead of 1192 cc. Incidentally, *Hot Rod* magazine reported on another performance upgrade in April 1957: the Okrasa kit with dual-port heads and twin carburetors.

Leader of the Pack

Then, along came European Motor Products Inc. (EMPI). Based in Riverside, California, the company revolutionized the aftermarket VW industry, thanks to an extensive line of products and smart marketing strategies. The man behind this empire was Joe Vittone, who opened one of the first U.S. VW dealerships in 1954: Economotors.

Two years later, following a successful venture selling his own valve guides, Vittone launched EMPI, which specialized in VW parts and accessories. Until then,

Volkswagen instructed its dealers to discard cylinder heads when valve guide issues occurred. Vittone saw this directive as nonsense, thus the idea of salvaging the heads by installing guides of his conception.

Many other products joined EMPI's line in 1956, such as the aforementioned Okrasa heads/carburetor kit. It was followed in 1958 by more high-performance components made in Austria by Denzel.

In 1959, Vittone introduced the EMPI-designed front anti-sway bar for the Beetle, a year before Volkswagen installed it as standard equipment on its own models. Next came the camber compensator, which was a clever rear stabilizer device conceived to greatly minimize the risk of back wheels tucking under the Bug during hard cornering.

The long-gone Foreign Car Guide *featured a wide variety of Volkswagens, including some one-off creations. This customized sedan with fender skirts and a long roof rack was barely a year old when it was unveiled in the magazine's pages in 1962.*

SHIPSHAPE VW
MODIFIED BY RETIRED NAVY MAN

▶ When Chief Yeoman "Ron" Mack, U. S. Navy, hung up his uniform last October, after twenty years of active duty, it looked for a while as if things would be dull. The chief decided, however, to make all the changes he had really wanted to on his '61 VW and the project has certainly kept him busy as the accompanying photos show.

First on the agenda was the fabrication and fitting of gravel guards for both front and rear bumpers with a backup light built into the rear guard.

VW, loaded, ready to travel.

Right: Koffee Kombi, shown with door removed. It can be covered in leatherette, it may be painted, or simply left with natural wood finish.

Below: Fender skirts (hand formed), fitted and painted to match VW original color.

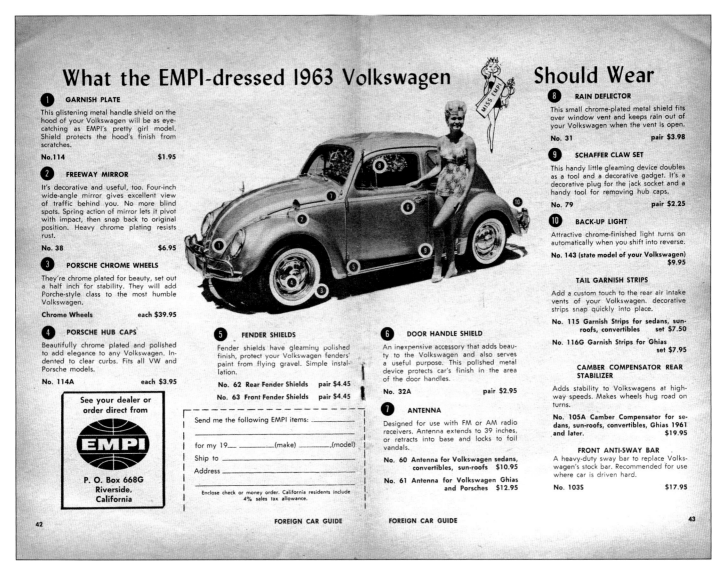

What the EMPI-dressed 1963 Volkswagen   Should Wear

1 GARNISH PLATE

This glistening metal handle shield on the hood of your Volkswagen will be as eye-catching as EMPI's pretty girl model. Shield protects the hood's finish from scratches.

No.114 $1.95

2 FREEWAY MIRROR

It's decorative and useful, too. Four-inch wide-angle mirror gives excellent view of traffic behind you. No more blind spots. Spring action of mirror lets it pivot with impact, then snap back to original position. Heavy chrome plating resists rust.

No. 38 $6.95

3 PORSCHE CHROME WHEELS

They're chrome plated for beauty, set out a half inch for stability. They will add Porche-style class to the most humble Volkswagen.

Chrome Wheels   each $39.95

4 PORSCHE HUB CAPS

Beautifully chrome plated and polished to add elegance to any Volkswagen. Indented to clear curbs. Fits all VW and Porsche models.

No. 114A   each $3.95

See your dealer or order direct from

EMPI

P. O. Box 668G
Riverside,
California

42   FOREIGN CAR GUIDE

5 FENDER SHIELDS

Fender shields have gleaming polished finish, protect your Volkswagen fenders' paint from flying gravel. Simple installation.

No. 62 Rear Fender Shields   pair $4.45
No. 63 Front Fender Shields   pair $4.45

Send me the following EMPI items: _____
_____
for my 19___ _____(make) _____,(model)
Ship to _____
Address _____
_____
Enclose check or money order. California residents include
4% sales tax allowance.

6 DOOR HANDLE SHIELD

An inexpensive accessory that adds beauty to the Volkswagen and also serves a useful purpose. This polished metal device protects car's finish in the area of the door handles.

No. 32A   pair $2.95

7 ANTENNA

Designed for use with FM or AM radio receivers. Antenna extends to 39 inches, or retracts into base and locks to foil vandals.

No. 60 Antenna for Volkswagen sedans,
           convertibles, sun-roofs $10.95
No. 61 Antenna for Volkswagen Ghias
           and Porsches $12.95

FOREIGN CAR GUIDE

8 RAIN DEFLECTOR

This small chrome-plated metal shield fits over your window vent and keeps rain out of your Volkswagen when the vent is open.

No. 31   pair $3.98

9 SCHAFFER CLAW SET

This handy little gleaming device doubles as a tool and a decorative gadget. It's a decorative plug for the jack socket and a handy tool for removing hub caps.

No. 79   pair $2.25

10 BACK-UP LIGHT

Attractive chrome-finished light turns on automatically when you shift into reverse.

No. 143 (state model of your Volkswagen)
                                    $9.95

TAIL GARNISH STRIPS

Add a custom touch to the rear air intake vents of your Volkswagen. decorative strips snap quickly into place.

No. 115 Garnish Strips for sedans, sun-
           roofs, convertibles   set $7.50
No. 116G Garnish Strips for Ghias
                                set $7.95

CAMBER COMPENSATOR REAR STABILIZER

Adds stability to Volkswagens at highway speeds. Makes wheels hug road on turns.

No. 105A Camber Compensator for sedans, sun-roofs, convertibles, Ghias 1961 and later. $19.95

FRONT ANTI-SWAY BAR

A heavy-duty sway bar to replace Volkswagen's stock bar. Recommended for use where car is driven hard.

No. 103S $17.95

43

See anything you like in this late 1963 EMPI ad? By then, the company had established itself as one of the main retailers of accessories. At $39.95, the Porsche 356 chrome wheels proved quite costly for the average VW owner.

Japan's Flat4 owns one of the largest collections of early EMPI components in the world. The team even displays some of the products' cool cardboard boxes with their distinctive orange and blue colors.

Takashi Komori, the founder of Flat4, began his search for 1950s to early 1970s EMPI accessories long before other collectors took notice of them. Check out the photo of the red EMPI Inch Pincher drag Bug on the left.

D'Ieteren, Belgium's official VW importer to this day, released its sporty Mach 1 special edition in 1964, though Volkswagen quickly put a stop to this independent enterprise. Mike Walravens and Fred Peeters respectively own these restored Ruby Red and Java Green examples. (Photo Courtesy Mike Walravens)

While not an original EMPI GTV model, Laurent Dubois's red 1967 Beetle received its GTV outfit during the 1980s. It includes a distinctive C-stripe decal kit along with 30-plus vintage EMPI add-ons: five-spoke GT wheels, functional side air scoops, and Delswift mirrors. (Photo Courtesy Laurent Dubois)

Vittone relied heavily on racing to put his company on the map in the 1960s, which explains the decision to alter his business's name. It became Engineered Motor Products Inc. With help from his talented son Darrell and engineering genius Dean Lowry, EMPI enjoyed great racing success during the decade most notably with an orange Oval Window Bug. It started its antics in 1963 as a circuit racer with Dan Gurney behind the wheel before becoming the most famous VW drag car of all time: the *EMPI Inch Pincher*.

True to the "Race on Sunday, Sell on Monday" saying, EMPI originated an improved version of the Beetle in 1966: the GTV. It came fitted with a variety of EMPI components with four different levels of finish from Mk1 to Mk4. The latter was the best equipped with such goodies as an anti-sway bar, additional gauges, a custom steering wheel, a carburetor kit, and British Racing Motors (BRM) magnesium wheels. There was a total of more than 40 changes.

As a side note, the Riverside-based VW giant followed in the footsteps of D'Ieteren, Volkswagen's official Belgian importer, which had released its own "tuned" Beetle in 1964. The well-appointed Mach 1, as it was dubbed, had a lot more to offer than factory Bugs: Porsche 356 wheels with radial tires, two additional VDO gauges, a 1300-cc engine boosted courtesy of Okrasa parts, and more.

D'Ieteren's endeavor was short-lived, since Volkswagen disapproved of a "sports car" at the time. Hence, only 28 (this figure remains uncertain) Mach 1s seemed to have been built in late 1964 and early 1965.

Looking back at EMPI's undertakings, both the *Inch Pincher* and the Beetle GTV (followed by the Karmann Ghia GTV and Type 3 GTV) served as remarkable promotional tools for the company. They greatly helped sell the rest of their more common accessories, including hubcaps, chrome add-ons, and walnut dash knobs.

The VW aftermarket was about to experience certain changes due in part to the arrival of a new breed of Beetles in 1968.

CHAPTER 2

THE POST-1967 YEARS:
NEW CAR, NEW ERA

The evolution of the Beetle was primarily dictated by technological advances, such as hydraulic brakes instead of cable brakes, and the desire to improve the driving experience with better seats, suspension, etc.

Volkswagen put less emphasis on stylistic alterations, which was a departure from other car manufacturers, American ones in particular.

Many automakers tweaked the appearance of their vehicles, occasionally in dramatic forms, simply for the sake of making changes. After all, the economy was improving in the industrialized world during the 1950s and 1960s, leading consumers to replace cars more often than ever before. People wanted the latest in design, and automakers battled to get their attention. The Bug could be considered an anomaly, as its overall shape had remained somewhat unchanged since its inception in the 1930s.

The untrained eye will likely see little differences between a 1967 sedan and an earlier model. The most drastic revision appeared in 1953. That year, the car lost its flat split rear windows, which were substituted for a single curved oval-shaped glass. This design endured until late 1957, when the body received a much larger rectangular window. More minor tweaks followed during the next decade.

Accessories
or
How to have more fun while driving your VW

Dated 1968, this cool 28-page Volkswagen brochure pertains solely to factory accessories available through dealerships. The 1968 Beetle, as seen on the cover, did not please all VW enthusiasts due to its bulkier bumpers that contrasted with its arguably more elegant counterparts used in prior years.

By 1967, Volkswagen had a well-sorted vehicle, which has since become a favorite among hobbyists. It featured a new 1500-cc engine along with many one-year-only parts, such as the decklid, which led to it being actively pursued by "'67 nerds." Some consider the 1967 as the best of the classic Bugs, being well finished and lively with its motor rated at 53 hp in the United States. The 1968 model introduced in late 1967

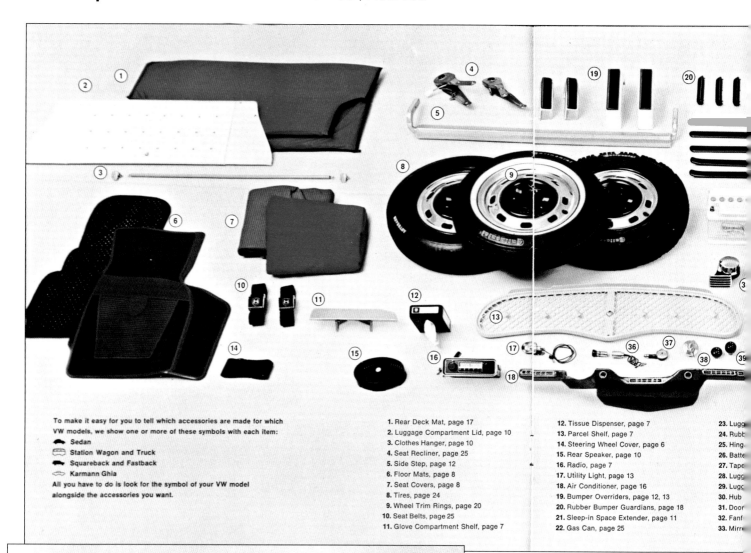

To make it easy for you to tell which accessories are made for which VW models, we show one or more of these symbols with each item:

🚗 Sedan
🚐 Station Wagon and Truck
🚗 Squareback and Fastback
🚗 Karmann Ghia

All you have to do is look for the symbol of your VW model alongside the accessories you want.

1. Rear Deck Mat, page 17
2. Luggage Compartment Lid, page 10
3. Clothes Hanger, page 10
4. Seat Recliner, page 25
5. Side Step, page 12
6. Floor Mats, page 8
7. Seat Covers, page 8
8. Tires, page 24
9. Wheel Trim Rings, page 20
10. Seat Belts, page 25
11. Glove Compartment Shelf, page 7

12. Tissue Dispenser, page 7
13. Parcel Shelf, page 7
14. Steering Wheel Cover, page 6
15. Rear Speaker, page 10
16. Radio, page 7
17. Utility Light, page 13
18. Air Conditioner, page 16
19. Bumper Overriders, page 12, 13
20. Rubber Bumper Guardians, page 18
21. Sleep-in Space Extender, page 11
22. Gas Can, page 25

23. Lugg
24. Rubb
25. Hing
26. Batte
27. Tape
28. Lugg
29. Lugg
30. Hub
31. Door
32. Fanf
33. Mirr

4. Utility Light
Illuminates engine and/or luggage compartment. Light goes on and off when hood is opened and closed.
🚗 🚗 🚗

5. Fanfare Horn Set
Let them know you're coming! Double-toned high pitch and low pitch horns let you sound a loud warning on the road. Heavy chrome finish. Mounts securely on front bumper. 🚗 🚗

6. Bumper Overriders
Here's extra protection for your VW when you're on the road and when you're parked. Chromed steel Over-riders have live rubber strips to cushion against shocks. 🚗

7. Rubber Bumper Inserts
These rubber strips run along your bumpers to provide an effective cushion against jars and help prevent bumper damage. Can be used in combination with Bumper Overriders. 🚗

felt a bit heavier in comparison because it was, having gained about 20 kilos/45 pounds.

Volkswagen cannot be blamed for the sudden weight increase. The company was simply at the mercy of the ever-evolving safety changes imposed by governments. As a result, the Beetle had to adopt bulkier, more angular bumpers that called for redesigning the hood and (again) the decklid, making it shorter than the 1967 version. The car addition-

Some accessories sold by Volkswagen came in handy, including the utility light, which was a smart way to illuminate the luggage or engine compartment. On the top left are the three icons that indicate the VW models that could benefit from this piece (Bug, Type 3, and Ghia in this case).

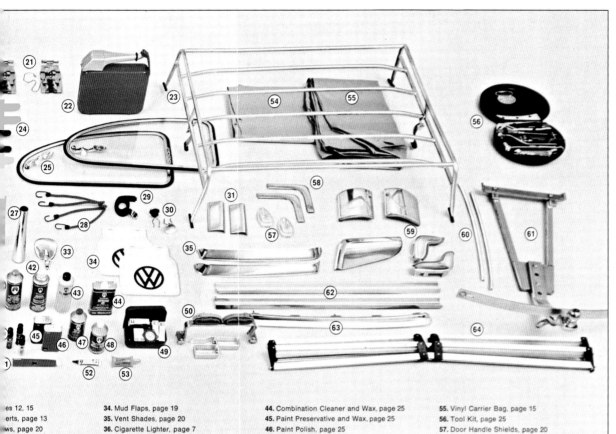

This spread gracing the 1968 VW brochure mostly displays add-ons for the Beetle (no less than 64 of them), though several could be installed on other models. Collectors will likely find desirable material here, such as seat recliners, a luggage rack, and a tool kit.

es 12, 15
erts, page 13
ws, page 20

ipes, page 20
ge 15
n Strap, page 15
'ool, page 20
ck Plate, page 22
age 13

34. Mud Flaps, page 19
35. Vent Shades, page 20
36. Cigarette Lighter, page 7
37. Tire Pressure Gauge, page 25
38. Gas Tank Lock, page 22
39. Gearshift Knob, page 7
40. Touch-up Paint, page 25
41. Windshield Washer Anti-Freeze
     and Solvent, page 25
42. Silicone Spray, page 25
43. All Purpose Cleaner, page 25

44. Combination Cleaner and Wax, page 25
45. Paint Preservative and Wax, page 25
46. Paint Polish, page 25
47. Gas Line Anti-freeze, page 25
48. Brake Fluid, page 25
49. Parts Kit, page 25
50. Ski Rack, page 19
51. Chrome Preservative, page 25
52. Molykote G Lubricant, page 25
53. Molykote Fluid Concentrate, page 25
54. Vinyl Tarpaulin Cover, page 15

55. Vinyl Carrier Bag, page 15
56. Tool Kit, page 25
57. Door Handle Shields, page 20
58. Door Corner Guards, page 20
59. Gravel Guards front/rear,
     pages 17, 20
60. Door Edge Guards, page 20
61. Trailer Hitch, page 14
62. Door Sill Protectors, page 22
63. Sunroof Wind Deflector, page 20
64. Ski Carrier, page 18

ally featured larger taillights and upright headlights, although the latter had already appeared on 1967s in the United States.

A Million Units a Year

True VW enthusiasts had mixed feelings about this new offering at first, as it was quite different from the simple lines they had come to appreciate. Eventually, customers warmed up to the novel design, and the manufacturer reported record sales all through the early 1970s with Bug annual production often surpassing a million units.

Accessories, such as radios, were typically special ordered by customers and mounted by the Volkswagen dealer that then delivered the new car. The Sapphire model was the most common in the United States. The same dealership could install an air conditioner with vents exiting under the dash.

1. Air Conditioner
Who says air conditioning is a luxury? When the weather turns hot, humid and just plain miserable, air conditioning is simply civilized. And you can enjoy economical, efficient air conditioning in your VW—because these units are made especially for VWs. Attractive, compact design blends with the dashboard, just as if it had been installed at the factory. What's more, these air conditioners are engineered to bring in lots of fresh, cool, dehumidified air with minimum horsepower requirements and no loss of leg room or luggage space. Pretty cool?

The unit is simple to operate, and features automatic temperature control, quiet 3-speed blower and large adjustable louvers that circulate the cool air in all directions.

3. Rear-Mounted Ski Rack
Here's a ski rack for all kinds of weather, all kinds of skiing. Made of polished stainless steel with leather straps. When you want to ski on snow, load up to 4 pairs of winter skis. When you want to ski on water, change straps (optional) and carry 2 pairs of water skis.

Smaller Rack
(Not shown.) Holds 2 pairs of winter skis or—with optional straps—1 pair of water skis.

4. Mud Flaps
True courtesy of the road. These mud flaps prevent the cars behind you from being sprayed with mud, road salts, etc. Decorative, too. Available also with VW emblem in circle.

What a great 1960s picture! Most items supplied by VW dealerships were conceived to fulfill specific purposes rather than being designed to just look pretty. A case in point: these mud flaps and ski rack.

More changes were about to come. VW engineers developed a new front suspension system with MacPherson struts introduced on the vehicle for the 1971 model year, and so the Super Beetle was born (as it is known in the United States). It can be recognized thanks to its bulbous front fenders, apron, and hood. Some of these cars came with a flat windshield (1971–1972, known as the 1302 in Europe), and others had a wraparound windshield (1973–1975 for the sedan and 1973–1980 for the convertible, known as the 1303 in Europe).

As a side note, American VW

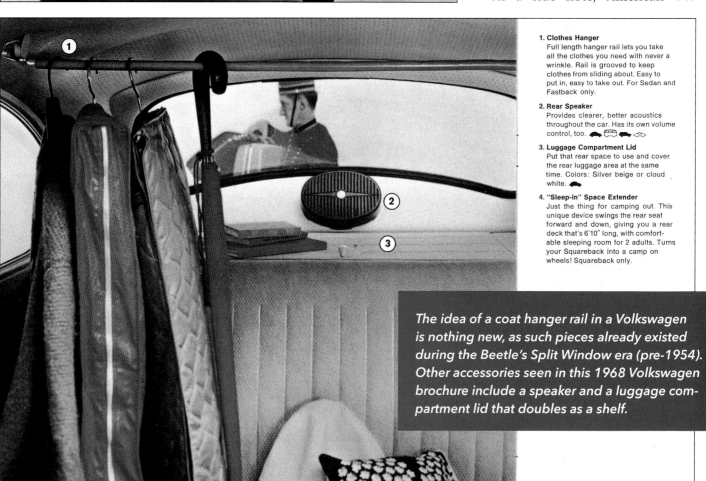

1. Clothes Hanger
Full length hanger rail lets you take all the clothes you need with never a wrinkle. Rail is grooved to keep clothes from sliding about. Easy to put in, easy to take out. For Sedan and Fastback only.

2. Rear Speaker
Provides clearer, better acoustics throughout the car. Has its own volume control, too.

3. Luggage Compartment Lid
Put that rear space to use and cover the rear luggage area at the same time. Colors: Silver beige or cloud white.

4. "Sleep-in" Space Extender
Just the thing for camping out. This unique device swings the rear seat forward and down, giving you a rear deck that's 6'10" long, with comfortable sleeping room for 2 adults. Turns your Squareback into a camp on wheels! Squareback only.

The idea of a coat hanger rail in a Volkswagen is nothing new, as such pieces already existed during the Beetle's Split Window era (pre-1954). Other accessories seen in this 1968 Volkswagen brochure include a speaker and a luggage compartment lid that doubles as a shelf.

From the Dunes to Baja

The 1968 Beetle featured a new four-lug wheel bolt pattern, thus calling an end to the larger five-lug rims in the United States. EMPI produced one of the first wheels to fit 1968-and-later models. Its design became an instant success and was copied by numerous other makers.

By 1968, EMPI had undoubtedly become the leader of the VW aftermarket industry, having more than 30 distributors in the United States and hundreds of agents nationwide. A resourceful art department led by Heinz Jung contributed to the company's success.

Jung showed multiple talents and was a stickler for quality, handling artwork and drawings, packaging and logo designs, catalogs etc. He also proved quite handy with a camera and was often assisted by another skilled photographer named Glenn Miller.

Company founder Joe Vittone remained on top of his game, unveiling a dune buggy dubbed *EMPI Imp* in 1969. It had pleasing lines rounder

enthusiasts are often not aware that the European market still had access to more basic and inexpensive Beetles through the 1970s compared to the United States. Take Germany for instance. In 1971, the 1302 sedan accounted for two-thirds of the model's sale, the rest being shared by the 1300 (20 percent), 1200 (10 percent), and convertible (3 percent).

Redesigns also affected other Volkswagens, the most evident being the Type 2 line (Buses). It is easy to spot a post-1967 version with clues such as a curved windshield (hence its Bay Window nickname) that replaced the split windows seen in 1967-and-earlier examples. This fresh and handy people mover shaped like a loaf of bread was 160 mm/6.3 inches longer than its predecessor and had larger side windows too.

While featuring efficient, modern independent rear suspension (IRS), it suffered from poor fuel consumption and remained painfully slow. Increasing displacement from 1600 cc to 1700, then 1800, and finally 2000 in the 1970s only partly addressed the issue.

New models meant new business opportunities for the aftermarket. Take the wheels for instance. Custom rims specifically engineered for Volkswagens had been available since the mid-1960s. However, changing the bolt pattern to 4x130 mm on most models led to the manufacture of newly designed wheels. In fact, EMPI was quick to release the four-lug Sprint Star and the GT Spyder (better known as the "8-spoke EMPI" within the VW scene).

than the world-famous Meyers Manx, which was created by Bruce Meyers in 1964 and recognized as the first fiberglass buggy. Car guys and girls are familiar with the dune buggy's concept, which is typically based on a Beetle floor pan (shortened or not) and complete with VW suspension and an air-cooled powerplant.

Bruce Meyers, who passed away in 2021 at the age of 94, built only 5,280 of the original Meyers Manx kits until his company closed in 1971. However, he estimated that his original design led to the fabrication of 350,000 copies or lookalikes worldwide. That is a staggering figure.

Although not the subject of this book, the dune buggy scene had become gigantic during the second half of the 1960s. The publishing world surfed the wave as well with *dune buggies and hotVWs* magazine being the most prevalent example. Launched in 1967 and still printed today (readers simply call it *hotVWs*), its content heavily catered to the buggy and off-road crowd at first. It slowly evolved to feature a wider range of air-cooled Volkswagens during the early 1970s. Advertisements consequently included an increasing number of accessories.

Folks who could not afford a dune buggy kit but still wanted to experience off-roading discovered a more affordable alternative: the Baja Bug. Its concept called for changing the shape of the fenders to allow the fitment of larger all-terrain tires and trimming/redesigning part of the body's front and rear sections to reduce overhang.

Gary Emory is generally accepted as the father of the Baja Bug, having built his low-budget off-roader in 1967 based on a 1957 sunroof Beetle. He and his father, Neil,

MUSCLE BEETLE

NOTHING IS OVERLOOKED IF YOU RUN THE GAMUT OF EMPI OPTIONS. TWO EXTREMES ARE POSSIBLE.

The ultimate VW street machine is one which combines style, luxury touches, performance and handling, all or any of which can be tailored to your personal taste in any degree.

Styling details include mag wheels, protective rubber bumper guards, chrome tail lights and front and rear fender shields.

Luxury items are most noticeable: wall-to-wall carpeting, wood-rimmed steering wheel, genuine walnut dash paneling and door trim, full instrumentation, rear parcel shelf with dual speakers for stereo, short-throw shift adapter and a console with two more speakers.

For performance you can add a street-legal extractor exhaust, two-barrel ram induction carburetion system, racing oil cooler sump, all highlighted with chrome fan belt guard, aluminum crankshaft and generator pulley with built-in timing marks to facilitate self-tuning.

Handling is optimized by racing shocks, a 16-mm diameter heavy-duty front anti-sway bar, heavy-duty rear anti-sway bar and wide-track stability.

For an ideal combination of performance and luxury, the GTV offers handling equivalent to a Porsche plus luxuries equivalent to sedans.

Graphics by Heinz Jung

...AS A BEAUTY

In 1970, Volkswagen Greats *magazine published this stunning spread with a drawing from Heinz Jung, EMPI's in-house artist, playing center stage. It drew attention to the EMPI GTV and its multiple specific parts, including suspension and engine upgrades as well as interior components.*

only used steel for their smart conversion. (Incidentally, Neil Emory was one of the founders of Valley Custom Shop, which produced some of the world's most beautiful custom cars in the 1950s.) Even Volkswagen took notice, using the vehicle in one of its tongue-in-cheek ads, with the slogan: "Is nothing sacred?"

By the early 1970s, the aftermarket had become aware of Gary Emory's concept, and Miller-Havens Enterprises led the pack. The California-based firm offered a $239.95 fiberglass kit with everything needed to transform a Beetle into a Baja Bug: four fenders, a hood, a bespoke front apron with two headlight openings on top, etc. Suddenly, such cars

EMPI did wonders with its marketing strategy, relying on colorful and comprehensive catalogs in particular. Laurent "El Dub" Dubois supplied these notable examples from his extensive collection of goodies pertaining to the brand. (Photo Courtesy Laurent Dubois)

The talented Bruce Meyers (1926–2021) was the brain behind the Meyers Manx dune buggy, which was set on a shortened Beetle floor pan. Some VW enthusiasts used the chromed tubular front bumper on their Bugs as well. That's Old Red*, the very first Manx, completed in 1964.*

could be found all over the Southwest desert. Even the National Off-Road Racing Association (NORRA) that sanctioned off-road competitions on the West Coast added a Baja Bug class in 1971.

Penned by the prolific Barry "Burly" Burlile in 1972, the Sandwinder was one of the most popular early Baja Bug kits. Its styling remains an off-road fan favorite to this day. Notice the redesigned fenders, hood, and apron with less overhang. (Photo Courtesy Barry Burlile)

Other companies released their own kits as years passed, including Sandwinder in 1972. Its version, imagined by longtime enthusiast Barry "Burly" Burlile, marketed a different design with headlights installed in the front fenders. To this day, Baja Bugs still have a strong following, being simple, efficient, inexpensive, and dependable when properly maintained.

Getting a Piece of the Pie

When it came to the street scene, some companies producing accessories became notorious through the years. A few of them remain currently active, such as CB Performance (a.k.a. Claude's Buggies Inc. when it started as a wrecking yard/repair shop in the mid-1950s), Scat Enterprises, and Gene Berg Enterprises. The latter were both founded in the 1960s.

Other firms came from a background dominated by V-8-powered domestic automobiles. Holley offered a carburetor kit called Bug-Spray for instance, while Edelbrock had a manifold for it. Add to the list Hurst and its sporty VW shifters, and Mr. Gasket and its distributor dubbed Super BugSpark.

Among certain VW fans, speculation revolves around the idea that the German manufacturer frowned upon companies that marketed parts with a performance edge supposedly because these components went against the image it had fostered for decades. The Beetle was supposed to be a reliable and family friendly automobile—not a hot rod. Some folks even surmise that Volkswagen of America put pressure on EMPI to stop selling the GTV to VW dealers for this very reason.

Well, I don't buy it. VWoA likely had a good understanding of the youth market and its desire to modify cars in the land of hot rods and customs. To prove the point, the automaker sold a range of sports-oriented, dealer-installed accessories in the United States from 1965/1966 until 1973. They were gathered under the Formula Vee name.

The Formula Vee was a popular VW-powered single-seat racing series. Starting with simple stripe kits to dress up the Beetle's body, the line expanded over the years to include products that could compete against EMPI's own offerings: custom wheels, a hood scoop, performance exhaust system, walnut instrument panel, tachometer, three-spoke steering

Hurst has played an essential role in the high-performance aftermarket automotive industry since the late 1950s, thanks in great part to its shifters destined for domestic vehicles. Yet, the firm also supplied models for Volkswagens, a.k.a. the "Hurst/Wagen."

Blaine Braziel drives a striking 1970 Bug loaded with Formula Vee equipment. The name referred to an extensive options package available in the United States via VW dealers that additionally offered to install them. Braziel's ride received "Formula Vee" stickers, Riviera-style mag wheels, a hood scoop, a fender guard set, horns, flared exhaust tips, and more. (Photo Courtesy Blaine Braziel)

wheel, Formula Vee body badge, etc.

Of course, these items were available in parallel to Volkswagen's regular accessories, which is illustrated in the photos at the beginning of this chapter. From tow bar and roof rack to carpet kit and pop-out side windows, VW dealers had it all. However, the market soon saw a major change.

In 1971, Filter Dynamics International acquired EMPI, although it became quickly apparent that the large company did not have a good understanding of the VW market. EMPI was gone by 1974/1975. Another firm later purchased the name, and it reappeared in advertisements during the second part of the 1980s. EMPI remains one of the largest worldwide purveyors of VW accessories to this day.

An ad published in the May 1969 issue of Rod & Custom magazine shows the "newest & greatest thing going on the Volkswagen street scene": EMPI's 2+2 Rally seats. Both the front bucket and rear bench seats were made of fiberglass dressed with snap-on vinyl upholstery.

The Legendary Bug-Ins

To find out about the latest accessories, enthusiasts relied on printed matter first and foremost. The U.S.-based *Foreign Car Guide* and *hotVWs* magazine were used in particular. VW shows were another way of discovering the latest products thanks to vendors and like-minded folks who had already installed them on their cars. It should be said that such events remained few and far between until 1968.

In October, promoter Vic Wilson launched Southern California's First National Bug-In, which took the scene by storm. The affair was held twice a year at Orange County International Raceway (OCIR) and had it all: a car show, drag racing, slalom, and off-road competition.

Through the 1970s, the event blossomed under the

California's Bug-Ins held from 1968 until 1983 helped shape the American VW scene. This 1970s car show photo reveals the range of accessories available back then: sun visors, sunroofs, custom wheels (often sticking out from the fenders), and flared fenders.

Could this be a real Split Window Beetle? Seen in the parking lot of a Bug-In, little is known about this pre-1965 yellow sedan. The two windows might have been grafted. Check out the decklid scoops and the post-1967 bumpers. Flared fenders cover wider tires circling what appeared to be chromed Appliance rims.

With slotted wheels, wider fenders, a side pipe, and an intricate paint job, this Bug nicely represents the pre-1975 U.S. custom VW scene. While we take lowered suspension for granted today, very few Beetles rolled with their nose close to the asphalt at the time, as demonstrated by the California Special.

Vans had a huge following during the 1970s, and Volkswagens were not spared from the craze. This example mixes period-correct elements that might be expected: a groovy paint job with "Keep on Truckin" lettering, E.T. wheels mounted with adapters, and truck mirrors and air scoops on the sides; it's all there.

watchful eye of Rich Kimball, who is a popular figure within the hobby to this day. Customs had a strong following as fiberglass components became especially popular before 1975, including wider fenders, trick hoods and decklids, scoops, etc. In this chapter, you can see several examples of these colorful creations that are often adorned with intricate paint jobs.

As the meet continued to grow, getting a good spot in the car show or the racers' pits proved to be a challenge as years passed, which enticed participants to sleep overnight in front of the gates. Rich Kimball made a few notable tweaks during the 1970s and early 1980s, including the addition of the "America's Most Beautiful Volkswagen" award.

Occasionally, the latter took the shape of half a Weber 48IDA carburetor mounted on a carved wooden base. It was a beautiful and desirable piece. Other changes in the program included the Bug-In Queen and King contests, in addition to the Engine Pull challenge. It involved two-men teams that had to remove and refit the engine of a Beetle and drive it across a finish line. The record stood at an astonishing 2 minutes 33 seconds.

Sadly, by October 1983, the party was over after 31 events mainly due to land development. An industrial park now sits on this prime piece of real estate, which is located near the intersection of the 5 and 405 freeways when driving toward San Diego.

It took another 22 years for the 32nd Bug-In to return to Southern California, mostly using the quarter-mile drag strip of Fontana. To this day, the happening remains a staple of the VW scene with its format inspiring promoters all over the world from Belgium to Japan.

A New Kid in Town

The Bug-In's post-1974 era brought some interesting changes. A new style of customized Volkswagens appeared at events, especially on the West Coast. It became known as the California Look, or Cal Look for short. Rather than adding accessories, this breed put emphasis on high-performance engines and clean lines, following the "less is more" motto.

If anything, owners would remove items from their vehicles, such as body moldings and bumpers, the latter

By the mid-1970s, a new kind of custom Volkswagen began to emerge. The California Look, as it was named, revolved around a simple, uncluttered appearance and placed less emphasis on add-ons as exemplified by Keith Goss's beautifully chopped 1962 Beetle. The trend called for a dechromed shell (vent windows included), moderately wide wheels (Porsche 911 models in this case), and very few accessories.

The California Look took its inspiration in the drag Bugs of the time with Lee Leighton's very successful 1955 Oval Window model being a perfect example of the genre. Amid the shared minutiae (a healthy engine, nose-down attitude, trim-less body, and lightweight wheels), magnesium BRMs such as these remain highly sought-after to this day.

being occasionally replaced with diminutive nerf-bars or T-bars. California Look cars essentially emulated the simple, lightweight racing VWs seen at local drag strips. My friend Bill Schwimmer, a member of Der Kleiner Panzers (a well-known Cal Look VW club), jokingly uses this punk rock analogy to describe the style: "Cal Look is like a Ramones concert: fast, fun, loud, and a little dangerous."

The days of accessories were far from over. From the late-1970s to the 1990s, *hotVWs* magazine featured page after page of massive ads from numerous accessory purveyors, including Small Car Specialties, Johnny's Speed & Chrome, Car Custom, and Auto-Haus.

The classic VW scene came to embrace accessories in recent times with clubs, such as Rare Vintage Air, actively seeking the most unusual pieces to dress their rides. Although leaning toward the custom side, other groups akin to the German Folks Klub heavily deck their Vee Dubs with an eclectic range of rarities too. You can discover a handful of them in Chapter 11.

Laurent "El Dub" Dubois is a longtime collector of 1960–1970s Volkswagen-related memorabilia, and some of it is associated with Auto-Haus, a chain of Southern Californian VW stores. Auto-Haus sold a wide array of accessories, as seen here displayed with catalogs and shirts. Legendary artist Dave "Big" Deal designed a large portion of the artwork. (Photo Courtesy Laurent Dubois)

WHENEVER HIGH PERFORMANCE IS SPOKEN -

AUTO-HAUS IS THERE!

Auto-Haus is the largest distributor of VW high performance parts as well as accessories for 4-wheel drives and vans. Send $2 for catalog to cover handling cost.
P. O. Box 428
Buena Park, Calif. 90621

The Auto-Haus saga spread from 1968 until 1984 when the company called it quits. This ad appeared on the back cover of the first issue of VW Trends magazine (1976). It showcased the new breed of California Look Volkswagens equipped with a set of chromed Porsche 356 wheels.

CHAPTER 3

EXTERIOR DETAILS:
DRESSED UP AND READY TO GO

Although the Beetle sedan's Deluxe version was better equipped than its Standard counterpart, either model remains a great canvas for any VW enthusiast eager to add a touch of practicality and/or glamour to his or her car, courtesy of vintage accessories.

Let's not forget about the convertible (often referred to as a cabriolet, which is the French word for convertible), which was another Bug version introduced in mid-1949 within the VW scene.

The German manufacturer offered two topless versions: one assembled by the Karmann factory (Type 15) and the other by Karosserie Hebmüller (Type 14). Both were based on the Deluxe/Export model. Karmann's version had undoubtedly more than a hint of the convertible seen during the 1938 cornerstone ceremony for the new KdF-Wagen factory. (As mentioned in Chapter 1, the event involved three prototypes: a hardtop sedan, a sunroof sedan, and a convertible.) Adolf Hitler was seen riding shotgun in the convertible's passenger seat that same day.

More than a decade later, Volkswagen selected Karosserie Karmann for its production cabriolet. This was due in great part to its excellent

Mike Malamut owns an incredible car collection, which includes a variety of vintage Volkswagens. His Mittelblau Metallic 1955 Cabrio features rare accessory bumper guards (supporting fog lamps) and Albert mirrors.

It's a pretty car, isn't it? That's a sought-after early Heb-müller Type 14A owned by Dan Arena. The New York resident mounted a handful of period add-ons, such as fender skirts and a Speedy side mirror.

knowledge of coachbuilding, having created its first automobile bodies during the very early 20th century.

The firm conceived a well-thought-out topless automobile, which still retained the inimitable round shape of the Beetle with the top closed. The top employed multiple layers of materials stretched over a steel and wooden frame. This made the interior surprisingly quiet and watertight, a notable feat in 1949 when a lot of other convertible makers struggled to keep vehicles leakproof.

Over the years, cabriolet owners have praised this VW model for being well built and great to drive, due in part to its construction making it torsionally stiff. Indeed, it featured plenty of reinforcements, although this led to extra weight as one might expect. A convertible added an extra 70 kilos/155 pounds compared to its sedan counterpart in 1957 for instance, thus some folks felt that the car had a sluggish feel when driving.

To be heard on the road, Bosch offered these louder-than-stock horns that look quite fancy dressed in chrome. They came with brackets that allowed owners to install them easily on bumpers.

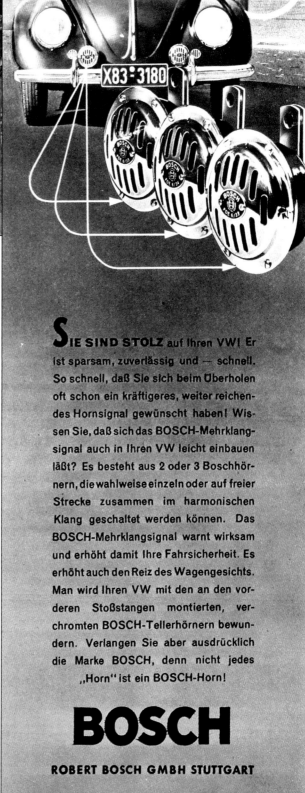

Desirable Decklid

Karmann's cabriolet came equipped with a handful of components unique to the model, such as the decklid. On the sedan, an air inlet destined to cool the motor resides below the rear window, while no such provision exists on the convertible due to the design of the top. This forced Volkswagen to conceive of an engine lid that incorporates vents in the shape of slits—either vertical (until 1957) or horizontal (1958 and later).

For Beetle sedan owners, the vents have become an accessory of sorts over the years. They allow more air to circulate around the engine and thereby improve its cooling, which is a welcome feature when running a high-performance flat-four that begs for additional fresh air.

Besides the Karmann version, Volkswagen also marketed the Hebmüller Type 14 cabriolet, characterized by its long decklid and 2+2 seat arrangement. The coachbuilder had a second VW contract to manufacture 275 police cars known as Type 18A. Most of these four-seat convertibles came equipped with detachable canvas doors, making entry/exit easy from the front seats and the back bench.

Sadly, Hebmüller's commercial agreements were short-lived due to a fire that destroyed the factory in July 1949. The company never managed to recover from the catastrophe. Only 696 cabriolets rolled out of the assembly line. Surprisingly, more than 150 of them are known to exist today, according to the Hebmüller Registry. In the meantime, Karmann experienced much greater success with manufacturing continuing through early 1980. Of course, other VW models can be neatly accessorized too.

Patina cars have a strong following within the VW scene, as is exemplified by this Split Window Bug built in late 1951 or early 1952 that is decked with a roof rack (one of the oldest VW accessories), ski rack, and mudflaps.

Dave "Pip" Pipoly (pictured) has restored and customized a number of early Volkswagens through the years, such as this 1952 sunroof model.

Dave Pipoly picked several accessories to dress the exterior: pop-out windows, Porsche 356-style headlight grilles, and these rubber bumper guards.

Fresh Air

When it comes to the Beetle, the most popular extra for sedans might be the side pop-out windows. Part of their appeal lies in their usefulness, as sedans came with static glass on each side of the rear bench seat (where it gets hot in the summer!). The convertible was fitted with roll-down windows.

Old pop-outs that still have their VW logo are especially sought after. They come in two main versions in the United States: 1964 and earlier, and the larger 1965 and later (which will also fit Mexican Bugs built until 2003).

Pop-outs prove efficient on sunroof-equipped VWs, as it allows the air to somewhat escape from the cockpit with the top open, making for a more comfortable driving experience by quieting down wind noise. Another option with the same aim consists of installing a deflector, which mounts in front of the sunroof. The deflector is available for Beetles with a soft top (ragtop) or a steel sunroof (starting in 1964). These items could be purchased as far back as the 1950s, although enthusiasts also have access to reproductions today.

Several other accessories came out of practicality, if not necessity, as demonstrated by certain turn signal offerings. Until early 1955 in the United States and 1960 in Europe, Beetles used semaphores (i.e., "arms") to indicate the driver's intention to turn. The semaphores popped up from the body and lit up when activated. Their bulbs did not flash. Germans called them *winker* and Brits *trafficators*. They were located in the B-pillars on sedans and below the waistline on convertibles.

An ad in 1956 from a company called Jokon appeared in *Gute Fahrt* magazine, showing true flashing turn sig-

Many automakers had already discontinued semaphores by the mid-1950s. To keep up with trends, Jokon sold these parking lights/turn signals in 1956. They fit over the semaphore openings.

The aftermarket began supplying pop-out windows with smooth frames (such as these) around 1951/1952. Volkswagen followed suit in late 1957 with its own version with grooved frames.

nals. They fit over the semaphore openings as a way of making a Bug both safer and more modern.

Then, in 1961, after flashing turn signals had become the automotive norm, the German government mandated that all older cars had to be converted to flashing turn signals. Jokon came to the rescue again, supplying a kit with four indicators that mounted on the front and rear fenders.

In 1961, the Beetle adopted larger taillights with integrated turn signals on top. However, it should be said that both Italy and Australia employed unique rear lighting (starting in 1958 and 1961, respectively) to satisfy local legislation requiring flashing indicators. Known as 50/50 models within the VW hobby, the upper half was amber, and the lower half was red. They might appear to be identical to the 1962-and-later taillights we all know (at least to the untrained eye), but they are actually slightly smaller.

As a side note, Europe used amber and red taillight lenses starting in 1962 (Germany in May 1961), while

All Bugs were equipped with blinking turn signals by 1962. This inspired (or forced) some owners of older models to update their cars. Jokon provided a kit with blinkers to be fitted on the front fenders and over the semaphores.

the United States retained all-red versions. Folks have chosen to use one or the other to personalize their cars for years.

For the Practical Individual

Numerous accessories flooded the market in the 1950s, and listing them all would be impossible. If truth be told, the format of this book often makes it difficult to present them in their respective chapters, as so many have been made over time. However, don't worry, many of them can be found through the rest of this printed work, mixing practical and ornamental items.

In the "practical" category, fog lights come to mind, along with roof and ski racks. The vent shades, which affix to the top of the doors' window openings, have been popular as well. These deflectors allow the occupants to roll down the glass partway

Besides being an original equipment manufacturer (OEM), the German firm Hella also supplied accessory horns along with lights that were sometimes chromed.

This color photo shows one of the Hella lights mounted on a Reseda Green 1952 convertible.

Sweden's Ulf Kaijser made quite a splash with his 1956 Oval Window Beetle during the 1980s. It came with numerous rare accessories: fender guards, door-handle guards, door vent shades, a shoe scraper (on the running board), tailpipe connector, Judson supercharger, etc.

When Volkswagen released its 1968 model, customers could order various accessories, including wheel trim rings, fender guards, tapered exhaust tips, and a sunroof deflector.

without being affected by wind or rain. They can be seen in the 1968 VW brochure displayed in Chapter 2. That same leaflet gives a glimpse of the eclectic assortment of handy exterior accessories available through VW dealerships: roof racks, bumper guards, mud flaps, trailer hitches, sunroof wind deflectors, etc.

Other products were used to protect the body. They came in the shape of aluminum guards. The finger guards, located under the outside door handles or hood handle, protect the paint from fingernail scratches. Vintage guards made by Robri in France remain the most popular.

The name of the company stems from the acronym of its founder, Roger Brillet, who started making automobile accessories in 1921 with most of them destined to decorate and protect a range of cars.

VW enthusiasts are still seeking Robri products today, especially the guards mounted on the front and rear fenders to shield them from gravel. (Note that some people occasionally blame them for not fitting properly when the issue might come from the fenders themselves, especially the not-so-accurate reproductions.)

Robri's shoe scrapers prove handy too. They affix to

the running board and allow folks to remove mud from their shoes before entering the vehicle.

Incidentally, the Robri brand still exists today, with a small workshop making quality hand-polished aluminum items using the same techniques as decades ago (see belles-anciennes.fr).

Making It Personal

Most exterior accessories manufactured back in the day had another purpose: to enhance the VW's appearance. It was also a great way for enthusiasts to personalize their cars. Some firms supplied different hubcaps, for example, others beauty rings (a.k.a. wheel trim rings) that fit around them and thereby hid part of the factory rims. Of course, many companies have been producing custom wheels since the 1960s—so much so that a complete chapter of this book is devoted to the subject.

Depending on the market, Beetles came with a variety of outside mirrors. They were typically installed by dealers due to the risk of being broken off while in transit from the factory. Some individuals elected to install aftermarket models, such as those offered by Albert. Today, the brand is mostly remembered for its swoopy mirrors (now reproduced) that fit on the front quarter panels just ahead of the side molding.

Speaking of moldings, Australian fans of Beetles occasionally customized their 1950s and 1960s models with additional side trim pieces sold as a kit, known today as

Several companies made outside mirrors for Volkswagens. The version marketed by Speedy can be easily recognized due to its round shape.

Aussie Flash Trim (check out the blue convertible in the last chapter of this book for a great example). They gave a sense of luxury to the humble German car as did various ornaments that slid over the hood's aluminum trim. One of them, mounted close to the windshield, was shaped like a wing with the purpose of deflecting rain, snow, and bugs past the windscreen. It somewhat worked.

Plenty of aluminum and chrome pieces brought some "bling" to the Beetle, such as the headlight eyebrows/eyelids, which are still some of the most popular accessories to this day. Tapered muffler tips made little or no difference in horsepower but gave a stock engine a more raucous sound. Other enthusiasts chose to install a chromed embellishment piece connecting both pipes (known as a tailpipe connector).

Not all aftermarket items ended up being as subtle as these small goodies. For example, take the rear fender skirts. These were an add-on that appeared on factory automobiles in the 1930s and became a widespread custom accessory in the 1950s. Skirts have a certain following within the VW circles today, especially the old variants offered by Foxcraft.

Volkswagen expanded its own range of accessories worldwide throughout the 1960s and the early 1970s. But in the United States, VW owners often shopped at JC Whitney, a popular source of replacement parts

Wheels have been a great way to personalize Volkswagens for decades, although choices proved limited until the mid-1960s. This is Ron Fleming's 1956 Beetle photographed in 1967 with friend Pam Bunch posing. The car sat on E-T rims. (Photo Courtesy Ron Fleming)

Collector Lloyd Kee owns a fleet of fantastic vintage Volkswagens, including a 1954 sunroof Bug loaded with uncommon add-ons. Check out the VIF mirror with integrated thermometer (in Celsius) that was likely made during the 1950s.

Dan Arena selected a handful of desirable goodies for his 1949 Hebmüller: headlight eyebrows, fog lights, a hood handle guard, Speedy mirror, and rain/bug deflector that fits ahead of the windshield.

Jokon conceived backup lights to improve safety, as was seen in this 1966 ad. The lights fit above the license plate of VW Type 3s as well as Beetles due to a few versions: pre-1964 and 1964-and-later.

and accessories for a wide range of automobiles both domestic and foreign. The mail-order empire had plenty of products for the Beetle especially.

American buyers often got add-ons from EMPI, which was an aggressive purveyor of dress-up and appearance parts. Company founder Joe Vittone certainly knew how to promote his line of products, having surrounded himself with a talented team. Along came the numerous fiberglass components mentioned in Chapter 2 from widened fenders to scoops featuring a variety of shapes. In the United States, Germany, or anywhere else in the world, dressing the exterior of Volkswagens proved easier as years passed, courtesy of a staggering number of accessories.

The 2019 European Bug-In at Chimay, Belgium, featured a terrific display of custom period accessories. In the showroom sat Laurent Dubois's 1970s-styled custom Beetle fitted with nerf bars and fiberglass components including the hood, fenders, and the window scoop. (Photo Courtesy Laurent Dubois)

The Long Journey: Eddie Galvan's 1960 Beetle Cabriolet

A project car is never finished. Ask Eddie Galvan, who has been making improvements to his convertible since 1991.

As this chapter pertains in part to convertible Bugs, it seems appropriate to introduce one of these not-so-common models. It is not only beautifully restored but also equipped with a variety of rare accessories. It belongs to Redondo Beach, California, resident Eddie Galvan, who became interested in Beetles thanks to his dad, who drove a 1971 sedan when the family lived in Venice Beach, near Los Angeles.

Galvan was inspired to purchase his own Volkswagen in 1991 because, as he recalled, "All my friends drove VWs back then, and we often cruised Hollywood Boulevard. I didn't have the money to get my own car. So, I got a job at McDonalds while still going to school and saved for almost two years."

After extensively scouring the local newspaper's classifieds, he found his 1960 cabriolet and then painted it black. A basic restoration followed about a year later, which included a few coats of the vehicle's original color, Paprika Red.

While it was often driven during the 1990s, the convertible saw only occasional use after the turn of the century. Galvan often thought about embarking on a second, more ambitious restoration. He finally took the leap in 2015 with the project involving some bodywork and a new, gleaming paint job still in the same Paprika Red color. Although the car had featured lowered suspension and Porsche wheels in the past, he decided to keep it all stock this time with era-correct 5.60-15 Firestone whitewall tires and grey vinyl upholstery.

Then, Galvan began his hunt for accessories. By his own admission, he may have gone too far at some point, as his convertible looked like a moving Christmas tree. But the vehicle now only features rare pieces, mostly manufactured back in the day in Germany. There are a few exceptions, such as the French Marchal fog lights and Italian two-tone front turn-signal lenses.

On the driver's side, the front quarter panel received a badge of Saint Christopher (the patron saint of travelers), which was an object offered by Volkswagen to owners who had traveled more than 100,000 kilometers. Other accessories on the outside include a Hirschmann red-tip antenna, Foxcraft fender skirts, and black and white mud-flaps.

Moving into the cockpit, check out the VDO trip speedometer, Dehne gas gauge, Sico flower vase, and more. In fact, Galvan estimates having two dozen desirable vintage accessories installed all over the vehicle.

An active member of the Rare Vintage Air car club devoted to original Volkswagens, Galvan also enjoys being an extra in movies with his cabriolet. Keep an eye open when watching *Once Upon a Time in Hollywood*, *Cherry*, and *Suicide Prevention*. It additionally appeared in a couple of advertisements, one for the Pep Boys store chain and the other for the Belgian Lotto.

The contemporary custom-made luggage was designed to fit behind the Beetle's rear seat. As a side note, Volkswagen offered the beautiful L452 Paprika Red color for its convertible in 1960.

There are some desirable pieces here. This Hella unit does double duty, serving as both a spotlight and a mirror. A second mirror made by Albert for VW convertibles bolts to the vent window's frame.

A number of companies supplied hood badges for the Bug. This one shows the coat of arms from the city of Rendsburg, Germany.

Koch's, a restoration shop located near Los Angeles, created the one-off banjo-style steering wheel. Koch's used the horn button from a Borgward Isabella, which was a car made in Germany during the 1950s and early 1960s.

The Akkord "Autotransistor" can be removed in an instant and used outside during a picnic. One of Galvan's friends found it in Germany during a famous VW meet held in the city of Bad Camberg.

The hard-to-find folding shifter came from a company called Volmac that is better known for its VW reclining seats. A porcelain ashtray slides over the shaft. Just make sure to empty it before you fold the shifter!

CHAPTER 4

INTERIOR DETAILS:
GET INSIDE AND GET COMFORTABLE

Motives for installing accessories on the outside of a VW are essentially twofold. Some, such as wheel beauty rings, may enhance the overall appearance of the vehicle. Others, such as roof racks, appeal to practical-minded automobile drivers.

However, when it comes to the interior, it is safe to say that most accessories belong to the second category in that they tend to serve useful purposes.

There are exceptions of course, starting with colorful plaid seat covers, although some owners installed them to protect the factory upholstery. Flower vases fitted on a Beetle's dash may not fulfill a specific practical need, either—well, unless you think the fragrance of flowers will greatly improve your driving experience.

Many interior accessories adorn the dashboard, which in itself often appeals visually to VW enthusiasts. In fact, let's digress briefly to describe the early Bug dashes, starting with the pre-October 1952 version. It is easily recognized thanks to its dual instrument pods located in the center, complemented with one glove box on the left and another on the right.

In October 1952, Volkswagen introduced a Beetle model incorporating numerous changes, including smooth bumpers, 15-inch rims instead of 16s, and a new dashboard. It only had one glove box (on the right side similar to most automobiles today) and a speaker grille in the middle.

Merry Christmas from EMPI! This 1965 ad displays a few of the company's most popular items: Cocoa mats, a Petri-style steering wheel, gauges, a radio, wood knobs, a padded dash top, and twin vents mounted in the quarter panels.

By 1950, several suppliers already offered radios designed for the Beetle, such as Schaub's Korsar model. At 385 Deutschmarks (about $91.45 at the time), it was not a bargain, as a Deluxe sedan cost just over DM 5,100 ($1,214.29) that year.

At the time, the Bug retained split rear windows, although they would be replaced with an oval-shaped glass in March 1953. (The car in question is being referred to as an Oval Window in the VW circles.) This dashboard design remained until the summer of 1957, when Volkswagen launched a brand-new Beetle characterized by a larger rectangular rear window. The driver now faced an instrument panel featuring one grille on each side of the speedometer and no more speaker grille in the center of the dash.

Must-Have Radios

When purchasing a Volkswagen, owners have often put a radio on top of their must-have list. Customers could list that option (at least from the 1960s onward) when placing an order. Yet, it should be said that the factory never installed them; technicians at the VW dealerships typically handled the job after the cars arrived. In some instances, the owner of the vehicle might have had the audio equipment mounted by an independent shop at a later date, or more rarely he or she fit it himself or herself.

The split-era Beetle's dual-pod dashboard welcomed a speedometer on the left and a blank plate on the right. It could be removed to install a radio or a clock. Philips produced some of the early sound systems in the late 1940s, specifically a model dubbed Elomar. Other brands followed shortly after, including Telefunken and its 1950 offering that was highly regarded by collectors due to its good looks. It had a chromed bezel with a stylized lightning bolt covering the speaker. Later, Telefunken units had a different design with push buttons.

Most radios made at the time came from Germany, as you might expect, from Blaupunkt, Schaub, Lorenz,

Henry Marchena's 1952 convertible retains an all-stock appearance, besides some suspension work and Porsche wheels. Notice how the Telefunken antenna resides in front of the windshield.

A range of valuable accessories equip Henry Marchena's cabriolet: an early Telefunken radio, a flower vase, glove-box doors with an ashtray and VDO clock, a locking shifter with an ashtray, cruiser pedal, under-dash reserve lever extension, Petri banjo steering wheel fitted with a Sun & Moon horn button, and an NOS horn ring.

The same rare Volkswagen also welcomes a restored Kienzle rearview mirror with a clock plus a desirable extension for the visor.

and Becker. However, Novak from Belgium also produced equipment for Split Window Bugs as early as 1950.

Beetles manufactured before October 1952 had a barely noticeable feature above the windscreen: a small dimple stamped in the body to affix the antenna. That's right, the antenna resided just in front of the windshield until Volkswagen figured that it would be visually less invasive if it was mounted on the front left quarter panel. Even certain antennas have fans within the collectors' world, especially the Hirschmann model with a red tip.

More radios entered the market during the Oval Window years (1953–1957). Blaupunkt had a strong following in Europe, while U.S. customers often selected a Motorola nicknamed Big M, due to the embossed M letter on the bezel.

Motorola and Blaupunkt remain the most commonly seen radios in Oval Window Bugs, but other brands produced lesser-known versions, such as this one from Becker.

This selection of radios photographed during a European Volkswagen meet in Le Mans, France, mainly features German models. Blaupunkt was a popular choice. Examples with black knobs are the most recent.

Accessory buffs hold the German Kienzle clock in high esteem. The "8 Tage" (eight days) inscription pertains to the fact that it will run for at least a week without the need of winding it.

In the early 1960s, American VW dealers began installing Sapphire radios. They evolved through the years, starting with the I (one) model and ending with the IX (nine) later that decade. Both Bendix and Motorola produced them. The Sapphire success story continued through the 1970s. The company equipped not only Beetles but also the rest of the VW line occasionally with different faces, bezels, and knobs.

Keeping Time and High Revs

Clocks have been another popular add-on, especially the Kienzle brand during the Beetle's early years. One version, which affixes to the rearview mirror's stem, remains a favorite with collectors. Other sought-after offerings came from companies such as Perohaus, VDO, and the lesser-known Kohler.

The Lufft Auto-Instrumente belong in the rarest-of-the-rare category, especially this rearview mirror that incorporates a thermometer and an altimeter. It's perfect for traveling on the Alps' winding roads.

Owners installed clocks in a variety of places, including in the center of the steering wheel (thereby replacing the horn button), in the speaker grille or the ashtray (on Oval Window Bugs), on the left side of the factory speedometer (it required cutting the Oval's dashboard with a hole saw), or in the glove-box door.

Other instruments served various purposes, most notably the tachometer. VDO has been a purveyor of such equipment since the 1950s, although the performance-minded American enthusiasts later came to appreciate AutoMeter's line of products in particular.

The company was founded in 1957 and first catered to the V-8 crowd. However, it caught the attention of VW gearheads during the 1970s. Since then, AutoMeter rev counters have been seen all over the world on both race and street-driven Volkswagens. Other known brands supplied tachometers compatible with 4-cylinder engines, including the affordable Sun models.

The list of aftermarket instruments would not be complete without a fuel gauge, as Volkswagen didn't offer any as standard equipment until the 1962 model

*Oval Window VW own-
ers often had to cut the
dash to install one or two
gauges, as demonstrated
by this 1953 Gute Fahrt
magazine advertisement
for Beck's Kraftstoffmesser
(fuel gauge).*

*Dated March 1952, this ad shows the Dehne fuel
gauge together with a Porsche 356 and a Split Window Volkswagen. The small instrument could fit both
vehicles.*

*MotoMeter from Stuttgart
provided a neat multipurpose
gauge that affixed to the
steering column. It kept track
of the fuel pressure, temperature (upper light), and fuel
reserve level (lower light).*

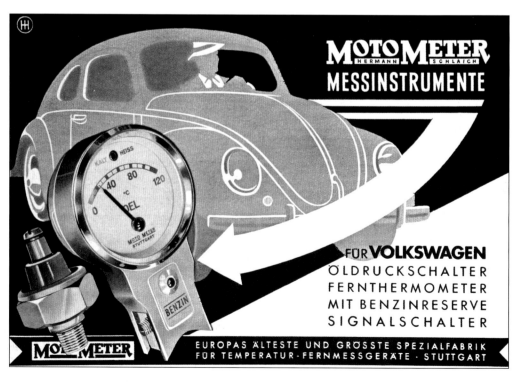

year. Independent suppliers did not wait to come up with alternatives. The pages of the March 1952 *Gute Fahrt* magazine show a fuel gauge produced by Dehne.

Founded in 1912, MotoMeter got into the game as well and conceived cleverly designed instruments. For example, its oil temperature gauge introduced in the early 1950s could clamp on the steering column with a bracket. MotoMeter later designed a three-gauge kit that replaced the speaker grille on Oval Window Bugs (1953–1957). These instruments have become highly collectible, although sourcing loose pieces, such as the matching sending units, can be a challenge.

EMPI unveiled diverse instruments as well, and its 1958 catalog featured a few gems. The Californian firm soon imported gauges from Speedwell in the United Kingdom (1966) and became known for its fully decked dashes. It incorporated a bunch of goodies bearing the EMPI name: gauges, radios, walnut dash panels, a wood

knob set, a soft padded piece that covers the top of the dash and integrates the grab handle, etc.

Steering the Bug

When it comes to steering wheels, one of the best-known brands remains Petri, which began advertising during the early 1950s in *Gute Fahrt* magazine. EMPI distributed a wide assortment of steering wheels from the 1950s through the 1970s as well. EMPI rims came in a variety of finishes, typically hardwood or simulated leather.

Most had three spokes (slotted, solid, or—in the case of the Formula—drilled), although a less-popular model inspired by the Porsche 912 wheel had four spokes. Known as the Riverside 500, it was introduced in 1966 and joined other versions sold by EMPI, such as the deep-dished three-spoke Petri imported from Germany.

VW enthusiasts often remember EMPI for its handsome 1960s and 1970s GT model, which is highly

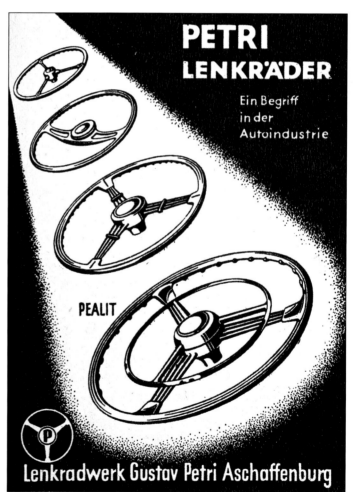

Fisher Products regularly advertised in the pages of Foreign Car Guide during the 1950s and 1960s. Besides distributing the Abarth brand, it also specialized in MotoMeter instruments, such as this 2-into-1 gauge (fuel level/oil temp) and a fuel gauge with a warning light.

Petri offered different VW steering wheels, as demonstrated by this 1952 advertisement, ranging from the basic (Standard Beetle at the top) to the fancy (banjo-style with horn ring at the bottom).

Today, like yesterday, collectors are hunting for beautiful vintage EMPI steering wheels. Flat4 of Japan owns this terrific selection, which includes several models with slotted spokes (known as GT).

regarded and coveted to this day. It featured slotted spokes and a diameter of either 380 or 400 mm. You might also see some of them with a padded horn button. Other steering wheel names had a certain following in the 1960s, most importantly Grant (introduced in 1962) and VW of America's wood-rimmed Formula Vee.

In fact, VWoA did not sit idle for long, releasing a variety of "sporty" products via its Formula Vee line. This dealer option package gave VW drivers the opportunity to add some

The interior of Blaine Braziel's 1970 Bug features a handful of accessories from the Formula Vee line available through VW dealerships during the 1970s, including a wood-rimmed steering wheel, a tachometer, and a shift knob. (Photo Courtesy Blaine Braziel)

Some Formula Vee add-ons could also be found in Volkswagen's more extensive general accessory catalog. This spread unveils the components available for the dash: a steering wheel cover, a radio, a cigarette lighter, a parcel shelf, a shift knob, a glove-compartment shelf, and a tissue dispenser.

1. Steering Wheel Cover
Enjoy a more comfortable feel of the wheel all year 'round. Vinyl surfaced Porotherm wheel cover keeps your hands warm in winter and dry in summer. Installs in minutes.

2. Radios

Sapphire AM Radio. News, weather, music at the flick of a switch.

Fully transistorized, no warm-up required. Push-button tuning to keep your eyes on the road, where they belong.

Sapphire FM/AM Radio. Your choice of the finest in radio programming while you drive. Quick, easy tuning with 5 push buttons. Chrome slide switch lets you change from FM to AM in a jiffy. Fully transistorized

with long-lasting silicon transistors.

Rear speaker available—see page 10.

3. Cigarette Lighter
Got a light? Sure you do—every time, with this automatic lighter. Easy, safe way to light up while you're driving.

4. Parcel Shelf
All the room you need for storing maps, gloves, cigarettes, what have you. Made of easy-to-clean flexible plastic.

5. Gearshift Knob
Custom designed of warm walnut.

Top shows VW shifting diagram. Shift in style.

6. Glove Compartment Shelf
Now you can find what you want in your glove compartment without fumbling or searching. Horizontal shelf keeps maps, books, etc. at hand. Vertical separators make three compartments for cigarettes, sunglasses, toll tickets and other small

items. Grey plastic with chrome trim. Slips right into place.

7. Tissue Dispenser
Don't sit there sniffling—have a tissue handy every time, with this practical dispenser. Black styrene with leather-grain etching and polished aluminum front plate.

Volkswagen never installed air-conditioning kits on its production lines. VW dealerships mostly handled the job. Check out the setup in Kim Martinez's fully restored 1966 1300 Beetle that was additionally equipped with a Sapphire III radio.

notable EMPI components include door pulls fitted above the door panels along with vents mounted in the forward firewall (or inside quarter panels) that were made to improve air circulation in the cockpit. Installation called for a hole saw more than 3 inches in diameter.

During the second half of the 1960s, EMPI continued expanding its range of products. A look at its 1966 catalog divulges Cocoa floor mats and a luggage compartment shelf behind the rear seat with a hinged access door in the center. When it came to seats, sports car fans occasionally opted for a pair of costly Speedwell G.T. buckets, whilst optional headrests for stock VW seats proved a lot more affordable. These are only samples of EMPI's offerings; more items continued to fill the company's catalog during the early 1970s.

flair to the interior, courtesy of walnut shift handles and knobs, a woodgrain dashboard kit embossed on vinyl, etc. They complemented the automaker's range of more practical items, including an air-conditioning kit with vents exiting underneath the dash.

Comfort and Protection

Seat covers also appeared early in German ads, thanks to companies such as Kamei. Another major player in the same country, Happich, distributed reclining seats and a long list of other interior-related items. In 1953, Happich advertised the following: sun visors, a dash grab handle, a steering wheel, floor mats, different ashtrays, flower vases, and more. (See ad in Chapter 1.)

Besides the aforementioned goodies, EMPI supplied its share of interior products, starting with aluminum guards used to preserve the paint from scuffs and scratches. Customers could install the guards on door posts (A-pillars), door sills, and door corners. Other

Germany's Kamei company marketed a wide assortment of VW products, such as upholstery kits and a 50-cm/20-inch-wide storage tray that only fits in front of the passenger. Note the armrest between the seats in a matching pattern.

a, b, c, d, e . . .
fünf Tips
für den VW

a) Der Schubladen-Ascher:
Die Ideallösung des Auto-Aschers für den Fahrer.
Keine Flugasche, keine Funken,
kein Stummelgeruch mehr.
Bequem von beiden Vordersitzen aus zu erreichen.

b) Der Haltegriff:
Eine Bequemlichkeit für den mitfahrenden Gast.
Stütze beim Ein- und Aussteigen,
guter Halt bei kurvenreicher Fahrt.

c) Die Leseleuchte:
Anstatt Ascher im Armaturenbrett einzubauen.
Ständig gutes Licht beim Kartenlesen
und Sortieren wichtiger Papiere!
Für den Wartenden gutes Licht für die Abendzeitung.

d) Der Windabweiser:
Beiderseits an den Lüftungs-Drehfenstern
anzubringen. Er leitet Zugluft ab
und durchlüftet den Wagen gründlich.

e) Der Fond-Ascher:
Der bequeme Seitenascher für die Gäste
auf den Rücksitzen. Formschön und praktisch!
Keine Funken können Kleidung
und Polsterung gefährden.

Wo Sie diese bequemen und praktischen
VW-Kleinigkeiten bekommen,
sagt Ihnen die Hersteller-Firma:

GHE

GEBR. **HAPPICH** GMBH
WUPPERTAL-ELBERFELD

In the 1970s, enthusiasts had access to an array of after-market shifters. From left to right are shifters from EMPI (SlickShift), Berg, Deano Dyno Soars (DDS), Hurst, and Cal Custom. (Photo Courtesy Mike Walravens)

Get in Gear

Several aftermarket suppliers addressed an issue often raised by VW fanatics: the shifter. While great for everyday driving, it wasn't the most efficient when trying to race at the traffic light due to its long throw and not-too-precise shift pattern. Kamei began marketing performance-oriented versions in the 1960s and so did U.S.-based businesses with EMPI being one of the leaders.

The company's 1966 catalog lists a smart device aimed at reducing the shifter's throw: the SlickShift, which consisted of a spacer fitted under the shifter. EMPI's advertisement stated: "SlickShift modifies the VW's shift-linkage mechanism to decrease by 40 percent the distance the driver's arm must travel as he shifts from one gear position to another."

By the late 1960s, VW afficionados had access to the Hurst shifter as well, which is a collectible chromed item, although a rare copper version existed as well. (Today's EMPI company has since reproduced the chromed Hurst with many parts being interchangeable.) Some folks elected to personalize their stock or aftermarket shifters with custom add-ons, ranging from EMPI's round walnut knob to a Hurst or B&M T-handle.

DDS came up with its own patented model as well that was redesigned by the respected Gene Berg in 1977. Berg covered all sorts of applications thanks to multiple

Smoking was big business in the 1950s, as demonstrated by this Happich advertisement featuring an Oval Window-era dash. The stock ashtray could be replaced with a unit that incorporates a courtesy light.

options: curved or straight shaft (respectively for 1956–1967 and 1968-and-later Beetles, although they are interchangeable), 40-percent or 60-percent shorter throw, shafts of different lengths (including a tall version for VW Buses), etc. Gene Berg Enterprises shifters remain a staple of the VW hobby to this day.

As can be seen from this list, numerous accessories produced for the cockpit have a performance edge. Check out Chapter 6, which is devoted to engines and ways to gain a few ponies.

Comic strips had a strong following in the 1960s, and EMPI surfed the wave with its "Archee the Accessories Salesman" character. This late 1963 Foreign Car Guide ad promotes EMPI's SlickShift.

Humberto Baca's 1957 Beetle Cabriolet

Originally built as a competitive show car, this 1957 cabriolet loaded with rare accessories now sees plenty of street use.

Many VW enthusiasts argue that the 1980s were the heydays of the show car scene with events, such as California's VW Jamborees, attracting the cream of the crop. Visitors could admire some amazingly detailed and occasionally outlandish vehicles that were built solely to compete in these meets. Owners would often display these trailer queens on jack stands with the wheels off to exhibit their chrome parts, painted brake components, etc.

Styles have changed since. Some of the wild alterations and pastel colors of the era have lost ground. However, this trick and fully loaded 1957 cabriolet would have

looked right at home with the best of them. Interestingly enough, a much smaller fringe of the VW scene had interest in vintage accessories in the 1980s compared to today.

Eric Goodwin, the man behind the build, has owned several notable air-cooled Volkswagens through the years, although this convertible represents his most ambitious project. The body required a ton of work before receiving a few coats of VW Ultra Maroon (L276) paint, a 1950s color slightly different from VW's Sepia Silver (L329) that was available on 1956–1957 cabriolets.

Looking at the pictures, some readers might exclaim: This isn't maroon . . . Fair enough, it certainly does not look maroon in the traditional sense, but that's what Volkswagen decided to call it. Goodwin then delivered the shell and chassis to his friend Dave "Pip" Pipoly, who runs a shop dubbed the Compound with Mike Davis and Bob Lacoste.

The team quickly went to work, bringing the car to the next level, using a range of coveted items, such as Bosch headlight glass and Hella turn-signal lenses. Other highlights include a front beam narrowed 6 inches by

Only a handful of accessories dress the exterior, including Flat4 impact strips on the bumper guards and a fog light of unknown origin. A narrowed axle beam explains why the Porsche 911 wheels are deeply set under the front fenders.

Did you notice the chromed speedometer and radio housings? Everywhere you look, the finish is outstanding. The neat window washer system with a clear glass bottle was made by SWF, which is a company better known today for its wiper blades.

The driver faces a Standard Beetle steering wheel with a custom horn ring that is complemented by a polished turn signal switch and a VDO speedometer with a not-too-common tripmeter option.

Old Speed, countless chromed parts, some components such as the steering box smoothed out (to remove any sharp edges), and four Airkewld disc brakes with Wilwood calipers.

The original, fully polished rims (measuring 15x4.5 and 15x6) were typically found new on 1960s Porsche 911s. Power comes from a 2276-cc motor fitted with a handful of desirable parts, such as original Weber 48IDA carburetors and a Vertex magneto.

While only a handful of accessories adorn the exterior, the cockpit welcomes a large selection of add-ons, especially the dash. Note the Saint Christopher badge and the Kienzle clock in the glove-box door fitted with an EMPI pull. The Gene Berg shifter and AutoMeter tachometer can be purchased new, although both brands have been

known by VW devotees since the 1960s and 1970s.

Goodwin unveiled his cabriolet during the 2016 VW Classic, displaying it in the spirit of the 1980s show cars: jack stands, two wheels off, mirrors under the car, etc. It looked fantastic. Shortly after, it caught the attention of Humberto Baca, who had to have it.

Fans of motorcycle road racing might be familiar with the name, as Baca has been involved in the field as a professional racer, a team owner, a team manager, and more. He also has a cool fleet of vintage Volkswagens, including a 1950 Split Window Bug. In his hands, the Ultra Maroon 1957 convertible has transitioned from a full-on show car into a fun weekend driver. Everyone can now enjoy seeing it on the road.

Some desirable Oval Window–era pieces are shown here. They include a three-gauge MotoMeter set replacing the speaker grille and a Motorola "Big M" radio. Note the MotoMeter clock holder on the bottom left as well.

Vintage Hüls reclining seat frames have been fully rechromed. As far back as 1952, at least two other German brands supplied recliners: Fritz Keiper and Happich.

While not specifically conceived for Volkswagens, the soda bottle holder looks right at home in this Beetle below the dash on the passenger's side.

CHAPTER 5

EMBRACING DIVERSITY: ACCESSORIES FOR THE ENTIRE VW FAMILY

More than 21 million air-cooled Beetles rolled out of various VW factories worldwide until 2003. This extraordinary success story led to the manufacture of hundreds of Bug-specific accessories, and many of them (radios, additional lights, steering wheels, gauges, and more) could be used on other VW models as well.

The vintage air-cooled family isn't only limited to the VW Bug, of course. For a change of pace, this chapter mostly concentrates on "non-Beetle" accessories, starting with the increasingly popular Type 2s, or "Buses," within the VW community. Assembly of the vehicle began in 1950 after a handful of preproduction units were built a year earlier. The Type 2 went on to become a big hit both as a workhorse and a people mover, as VW supplied an extensive array of versions.

When it comes to 1950–1967 Buses featuring two windscreens (known as Split Window Buses), the selection included several stark offerings, such as single-cab and double-cab trucks. There was also the Kombi, which was characterized by a cargo compartment finished in primer. The top of the line was the far better-equipped Deluxe Microbus, which had up to 23 windows, an aluminum body and bumper trim, a more luxurious interior, two-tone color schemes (with the exception of an all-white model), etc. Somewhere between the Kombi and the Deluxe Microbus was the passenger-friendly Microbus, which is frequently referred to as the Standard Microbus to avoid any confusion.

Considering the range of trim levels, some enthusiasts choose to accessorize their pre-1968 Type 2s by cleverly selecting a handful of factory

Shawn Madison from Tacoma, Washington, drives a well-appointed 1963 truck that Volkswagen could have built but didn't. It features details typically found on Deluxe Microbuses: a two-tone paint job, body molding kit, grafted Sekurit skylight glass, and a shortened Bus sunroof.

This Transporter sitting on Centerline-lookalike wheels incorporates particulars often found on customized Type 2s during the 1960s and 1970s from the side scoops to the wider rear wheels and tires. They explain the radiused wheel wells and fender extensions.

Safari windows remain one of the most popular Type 2 accessories. In this case, they have been complemented with a cyclops headlight from a pre-1947 Chevy truck. Notice the custom roof rack that follows the shape of the lamp.

Seen at the popular So-Cal Vintage VW Treffen event is a 1954 Microbus equipped with a Hurst bumper and a Behr-style fresh air roof scoop specific to pre-1956 Buses. (Later models had an overhang above the windscreen that ducted fresh air.)

Nur **BeKöWa**
Auto-gepäck-träger

in Spezialausführung
für VW-Limousine
und Kleinbus
Auch für die Schiebe-dachausführung alle
Größen vorrätig

Immer obenauf mit BeKöWa

Wenden Sie sich an Ihren VW-Händler

Hersteller: **Bernhard Körner, Hamburg-Wandsbeck**

Telefon 286704

Not enough space in your Transporter's cabin? The XXL-sized BeKöWa roof rack should certainly help. This ad appeared in the January 1954 issue of Gute Fahrt magazine.

components, typically coming from the well-appointed versions. This approach can result in interesting one-offs, such as double cabs fitted with Deluxe body trim, two-tone paint, and skylight windows—a model Volkswagen *could* have built. Such creations often feature windshields that tilt up to bring fresh air into the cockpit. Called Safari windows, they became an option in 1954, possibly even a year earlier. They were quite common in countries with a warm climate, such as Australia and Portugal.

Fans of V-8-powered domestic automobiles might be familiar with Hurst, a name typically associated with shifters. They gained huge momentum with muscle car and hot rod owners through the 1960s. A little-known fact is that the company had humble beginnings during the previous decade, producing massive tubular bumpers that would fit 1958-and-earlier Buses. Combining thick-wall tubing and flat stock, they bolted to the factory front and rear bumpers. The back unit proved much simpler in design. They have become very rare, although enthusiasts can now purchase accurate reproductions.

Type 2 Generations

Stating the obvious, Type 2s offered a lot more space inside compared to the Beetle. Yet, folks in need of more luggage or parcel capacity have installed roof racks on their Transporters since the 1950s. Based near Hamburg, BeKöWa was one of the first companies to get into that market, supplying a model that covered the entire length of the roof.

Speaking of the roof, Buses at car shows might occasionally be equipped with a third

Actuated from the cockpit, the SIMO electromagnetic engine lid hatch for Buses served as an efficient antitheft device. Very few are known to exist today.

1. **Luggage Rack**
   This rack gives you fast extra luggage capacity. Fastens quickly to the rain channel. Rubber-tipped feet protect the roof. Rack is made of silver-painted tubular steel. Available in various sizes.

2. **Side Step**
   Makes it easier to get in and out of your VW Station Wagon. Step is made of durable steel with aluminum cover. Installs easily in jack wells.

3. **Bumper Overriders**
   Help protect your Station Wagon or Truck from dents while driving and

when parked. Painted steel overriders have live rubber strips to cushion against shocks.

Folding Ladder.
(Not shown.) For VW Trucks and Station Wagons. Lets you climb to the roof for easy loading and unloading of baggage.

For additional luggage rack accessories, please see pages 14-15

Volkswagen of America offered an assortment of accessories, some of which are rarely seen today, such as this NOS retractable front step found on a 1963 Type 2 double cab. Installing them required drilling into the body.

This Volkswagen brochure highlights the Bay Window Bus and a selection of the most popular accessories to this day: a steel luggage rack fastened to the rain channel, sidestep installed in the jack wells, and bumper overriders with rubber strips.

swoopy headlight (nicknamed cyclops within the VW community) mounted above the split windscreen. This accessory of sorts requires a bit of explanation. Its origin cannot be traced back to a specific aftermarket purveyor but to American car manufacturers.

It turns out that 1941–1946 Chevrolet trucks in particular came equipped with sleek headlights, and their shape proves almost perfect for a Type 2 roof. The said Chevy lighting can be installed with minimal alterations, although some gearheads have found ways to adapt other units from 1930s U.S. automobiles as well.

The German automaker unveiled a new generation of Type 2s in late 1967. They were immediately recognizable courtesy of their one-piece, curved windscreens, hence the Bay Window nickname. Like its predecessor, customers had access to various trim levels. Both the Split and Bay Window Buses (manufactured until 1979 in Europe) could be equipped with numerous aftermarket accessories, from side steps to bumper guards not forgetting the well-liked and practical roof racks. Clients occasionally purchased a ladder, which made loading much easier.

Ghias, Type 3s, and Beyond

Other air-cooled models joined the VW family as years passed, such as the Type 14 Karmann Ghia (1955–1974). Due to its fairly low production figure, at least compared to the Beetle, few companies ventured into making accessories for it.

One of the most successful accessories could be installed for esthetic and/or practical reasons: the fake nose grille. Its shape took inspiration in 1950s Italian cars, such as Alfa Romeos, arguably a fitting add-on since the Type 14 had been designed by Carrozzeria Ghia in Turin. Some folks bolted it on because they liked its look, and others chose it to hide a dent that had damaged the nose of the vehicle just above the bumper.

In 1961, Volkswagen also introduced the Type 3, which was produced until 1973 and was available in four versions (not counting the convertible prototypes). They included the Notchback (three-box design), the Squareback (station wagon), and the Fastback (slanted roof, starting with the 1966 model year). There was also the sporty Type 34 Karmann Ghia, which stopped production in 1969.

Once again, Volkswagen smartly chose to offer various trim levels for its Type 3 line, as illustrated by

Ghia gash? Ghia Guard! From a 1964 issue of Foreign Car Guide, *Rande Company advertised a purely decorative grille that was custom designed to contour the nose of a Type 14 Karmann Ghia. It came in handy to hide a dent.*

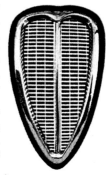

Volkswagen produced a little more than 42,000 Type 34s in 8 years, including Dan Finley's L554 Cherry Red 1965 model. He topped the front bumper with NOS Hella horns.

this chapter's 1964 French VW catalog spreads that shows a duo of Notchbacks. It is clear to see there is better equipment on the 1500 S compared to the 1500 (which was called the 1500 N in other countries).

The "S" featured bumper guards, wheel trim rings, side moldings, pop-out windows, and different lighting. Upgrading a basic Type 3 with parts from more luxurious versions has been a straightforward way to personalize this model since the 1960s.

Volkswagen supplied a range of Type 3 accessories through its dealership network. One of the most sought-after was the chrome bumper guards with protective rubber and matching bows, a kit reminiscent of the setup found on Deluxe/Export Beetles. Difficult to find today, the kit is now being reproduced and fits 1961–1969 Type 3 bumper blades.

Other add-ons popular with collectors include coco mats, mudflaps, specific gauges (such as the Type 34 6,000-rpm tachometer), and Albert mirrors. To this day, Type 3 owners also see fit to install side scoops fitting over the rear fenders' vents to draw additional air in the engine compartment.

Amid the VW community, collectors are actively seeking Hirschmann red-tip antennas, such as this NOS example found on Jurgen Magdelyns's 1968 Type 34 from Belgium.

For his black Type 34 fitted with a super-rare factory electric sunroof, Jurgen managed to find a range of NOS parts, such as these blinds originally manufactured for the Australian market.

Berline VW 1500

C'est une Volkswagen. On ne le remarque pas au premier coup d'œil. Mais à coup sûr au second. Elle est plus grande, plus rapide, plus confortable que la VW 1200. Elle est donc plus chère. Nous ne l'avons pas conçue aussi large et aussi grande qu'il était possible de le faire. Nous l'avons voulue raisonnable. Ce qui signifie : carrosserie de forme compacte, pratique et élégante.

A French VW brochure dated September 1963 highlights the differences between two Notchbacks: an entry-level 1500 and a higher-end 1500S. Among the disparities are bumper guards, front turn signals, taillights, wheel trim rings, pop-out windows, side moldings, and marker lights. For decades, Type 3 owners have personalized their vehicles by installing some of the more luxurious factory components.

Berline VW 1500 S

Cette voiture vous offre encore bien davantage. Primo : tout ce qui séduit dans la berline VW 1500. Secun... baguettes-enjoliveurs sur les côtés par exemple). Tertio : glaces arrière pivotantes, deux feux de stationnement, ... automatique des dossiers avant. Eclairage du coffre arrière. Tout ceci et bien plus encore fait partie de l'équipement de série (sauf la peinture deux tons fournie moyennant supplément). La VW 1500 S est donc plus élégante, plus confortable, mais aussi plus rapide : 2 carburateurs + 54 CV = vitesse maxi de 135 km/h. Refroidissement par air = vitesse de croisière de 135 km/h.

1. Ski Carrier
This versatile ski carrier can be mounted quickly on the rain channel or on the luggage rack. Skis can be locked in place with padlocks (not supplied).

2. Rubber Bumper Guardians
When you're parked, some of those big cars can really leave dents and scratches. Give your VW cushioned protection with the Rubber Bumper Guardians.

A happy family complements a Type 3 Squareback (Variant in Europe) that is equipped with a ski carrier and rubber bumper guardians, which is what Volkswagen called the bumper guards' rubber strips in this 1968 brochure.

More from the VW Line

Following the above-mentioned models, Volkswagen launched the Type 4 line in 1968 with the 411 being offered as two-door or four-door Fastbacks. A two-door station wagon version followed in 1969. They ran a new rear-mounted, air-cooled engine known under the Type 4 denomination, which displaced 1679 cc and delivered 68 hp. The vehicle was met with mild enthusiasm by VW aficionados due in part to its unconventional design.

Much larger and more expensive compared to the Beetle, the Type 4 faced an uphill battle from the get-go.

There was a German economy in a recession, new taxes, and fierce competition from foreign automotive manufacturers.

A redesign for the 1973 model year led to the VW 412, but again, sales remained sluggish. Only around 370,000 of the Type 4 models found buyers from 1968 until 1974, when they were discontinued. The aftermarket industry had little interest in the 411 and 412. Even Volkswagen offered few goodies for them—the most notable being a roof rack for the station wagon (identical to Type 3s) and an under-dash package tray.

In 1969, Volkswagen unveiled another quirky automobile: the Thing. It was known as 181 or 182 in different parts of the world, depending on left-hand or right-hand drive configurations,

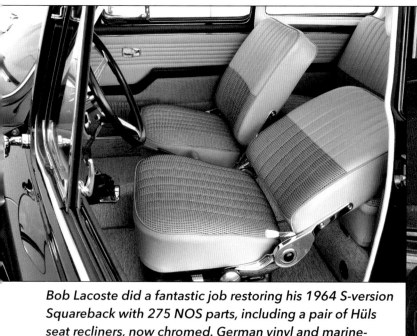

Bob Lacoste did a fantastic job restoring his 1964 S-version Squareback with 275 NOS parts, including a pair of Hüls seat recliners, now chromed. German vinyl and marine-grade mesh material cover the seats.

Founded by Karl Meier in 1949, German manufacturer Kamei went on to produce countless accessories, including the first Beetle spoiler (1953) and this throttle pedal cover.

This is from a 1968 VW brochure. The so-called Sleep-in Space Extender was described as follows: "This unique device swings the rear seat forward and down, giving you a rear deck that's 6 feet, 10 inches long with comfortable sleeping room for 2 adults."

respectively. The boxy all-terrain model, somewhat reminiscent of the World War II Kübelwagen, was produced from 1969 until 1978. Again, a limited number of accessories can be found for the vehicle with bumper over riders, hardtops, and push bars being arguably the most commonly seen.

As a sidenote, undoubtedly one of the most uncommon air-cooled Volkswagens remains the Type 147, which is called the Fridolin within the VW community. Both the German and Swiss postal services purchased most of the 7,300-or-so examples manufactured between 1964 and 1974. The strange-looking delivery van featured two sliding doors, a front evocative of Type 3s, and a back with traits akin to VW Buses. Apparently, no accessories specific to this workhorse exist on the market.

Idaho-resident Don McNeal personalized his rare 1972 Fridolin (an ex-German mail carrier) with altered ribbed Bus bumpers, VW semaphores, dual fog lights, and an accessory Type 3 (air vent) hood scoop.

Around the World

Volkswagen never exported the Fridolin to the United States; the few seen on this side of the ocean were imported by private parties. Other VW models have also trickled out of foreign countries to land on U.S. shores thanks to the grey market. Such is the case with the Type 3 Notchback and Type 34 Karmann Ghia, which were not offered by American VW dealerships unlike the Type 3 Fastback and Squareback.

In fact, many air-cooled models were manufactured specifically for the needs of certain countries. Most of these automobiles remain almost unknown in the United States. Mexico had the Hormiga ("Ant" in Spanish), a boxy two-door truck with both the engine and gearbox located under the cabin.

Other countries produced almost identical workhorses. Australia offered a VW Thing-like all-terrain vehicle dubbed the Country Buggy. Yet, Brazil remains one of the lands with the richest range of air-cooled Volkswagens: Brasilia (a small Squareback), four-door VW 1600, sporty SP2, and Karmann Ghia TC, Bay Window Type 2s with unique window arrangements, Gol (not Golf) with a front-mounted air-cooled engine, and more.

Overall, locating a few of the accessories unveiled in this chapter can be quite a challenge. They are often scarce compared to the countless goodies available for Beetles, as might be expected. But to some enthusiasts, finding a not-so-common accessory for a not-so-common Volkswagen remains pure joy.

Two uncommon gauges were photographed in Germany on a 1967 Fastback: a VDO rev counter and a VDO speedometer with trip meter. (The latter records the distance traveled during a short trip, as the readout can be reset to zero.)

Tracy Davis's 1966 Squareback

Locating accessories specific to Type 3s can turn into a challenge. Tracy Davis managed to unearth several of them, and they are now proudly decking his 1966 station wagon.

Type 3 owners rave about the vehicle's qualities from the roomy interior to the comfortable ride and good power. It's difficult to let them go once the sweet taste of the model has been discovered, as Tracy Davis will confirm. The Los Angeles, California, resident has had long experience with air-cooled Volkswagens starting in the early 1980s with a California Look 1971 Super Beetle (1302 in Europe). Other Volkswagens have followed since, although he has kept his 1966 Squareback the longest, having purchased it in 2000.

When found, the car's body featured only a handful of rust spots, while the factory L87 Pearl White paint still covered most of the German tin; yet, strangely, the hood appeared to have suffered from a fire. The automotive collectors' world did not talk much about preserving original paint and patina shortly after the turn of the century. Thus, Davis chose to have the shell resprayed in that same L87 color. Californian Type 3 specialist ISP West supplied an assortment of new and good used parts specific to the model, making the restoration easier.

While Davis appreciates bone-stock Volkswagens, he returned to his roots by adding some details typically associated with the California Look: a lowered suspension and a set of genuine 1960s EMPI Sprint Star wheels. Notice their 4x130-mm bolt pattern (because 1966 marked the first year Volkswagen employed four-lug wheels on Type 3s) complemented with disc brakes in the front and drums in the back.

I photographed Tracy Davis's Squareback in front of Pann's, which is an L.A. coffee shop landmark that opened in 1958. Davis went for an all-stock outside appearance except for the rims and lowering job.

The 1966 wagon seemingly received a couple of dealer-installed upgrades when new, specifically an air-conditioning kit and an aluminum luggage rack that was permanently mounted on the roof.

While Davis selected reproduction chrome bumper guards with protective rubber and matching bows (a.k.a. towel bars), both the gravel guards and EMPI Sprint Star rims are "the real deal."

Remember, customers could specify the accessories they wanted when ordering their cars from VW dealerships. These add-ons were installed by the dealership in question once the vehicle arrived at their facility. In the case of this Squareback, the client listed a couple of items: an aluminum, permanently mounted roof rack together with an air-conditioning kit. This was rare equipment even in its day because it was fairly expensive.

Davis elected to keep both of them, although part of the air-conditioning system had been removed from the engine before he purchased the wagon. The vents under the dash remain in place for now, as he might make the setup work again one day.

To further personalize his ride, Davis went on a hunt for additional Type 3–specific accessories. It was not an easy task, considering their rarity compared to their Beetle counterparts. Most had been manufactured in Germany back in the day, including the door-handle guards (different from the Bug's model), rear gravel guards, and a Hirschmann red-tip antenna. He also unearthed a pair of hooded mirrors produced by Albert, a company better known for its Beetle "swan neck" mirrors mounted on the front quarter panels. The cockpit houses a handful of desirable components as well: an original EMPI GT wood-rimmed steering wheel, an EMPI glove-box pull, a 6,000-rpm tachometer, and a trip odometer.

This Squareback came from the factory with a 1584-cc motor, but Davis fitted a powerplant with a bit more oomph instead. Replacing the 85.5-mm pistons and cylinders (typical of 1600-cc VW engines) with 87s led to a displacement of 1641 cc. He also swapped the factory

dual 32-mm Solex carburetors with two larger Weber 42DCNF units made popular by Gene Berg Enterprises. As an aside, adapting twin carburetors in a Type 3 can be quite challenging due to space limitation in the engine compartment, but these specific Webers fit perfectly once topped with low-profile Ram-Flo air filters.

Combining a lowered suspension with a more powerful flat-four translates into a nimble vehicle that happily zooms through L.A.'s hectic traffic and is an ideal cruiser to reach the So-Cal beaches. Also, adding a selection of rare accessories makes this Squareback extra special.

Better known for its "swan neck" mirrors for Beetles, Albert also produced these desirable Type 3 hooded units that bolt to the doors.

The air-conditioning system retains its vents and controls under the factory dash. They surround an attractive era-correct Blaupunkt radio, equipment popular in Germany back in the day.

So, you think vintage aftermarket seat recliners for Bugs are rare? Try finding a Volmac model for Type 3s. This photo shows how the mechanism can cleverly tilt back in an instant.

CHAPTER 6

ENGINE AND PERFORMANCE: PUTTING SOME MUSCLE INTO IT

Engine components in a book dedicated to vintage accessories? Why, yes! Take a pair of carburetors for instance. It turns out they might be a little more than just mechanical devices—at least to a fringe group of motorheads.

First, stating the obvious, properly tuned dual carbs add some *oomph* to a Volkswagen. Second, enthusiasts who tend to accessorize the exterior/interior of their Volkswagen will often feel the urge to find goodies of the similar period for the motor. It makes a project car more complete. Third, these same folks likely see beauty in specific mechanical components. Yes, beauty. Why could an Art Deco radio or a 1940s Wurlitzer jukebox be considered visually striking but not a pair of Italian 1960s Weber 48IDA carburetors nicely framing a curvy VW fan shroud?

To better understand the origin of high-performance VW engine components, lets travel back to the pre–World War II era. Ferdinand Porsche had just completed the Beetle (called the KdF-Wagen at the time) and unveiled it to a fanatical German crowd in 1938. The same Doctor Porsche was also put in charge of creating three KdF-Wagen-based race cars for the Berlin to Rome long-distance race. It was canceled as Germany went to war.

Built in the spring of 1939, the all-aluminum, lightweight, and very aerodynamic Type 64/60K10 coupe could reach a top speed of 145 kph/90 mph. That was quite an accomplishment at the time, considering that the engine developed 32 hp, which was certainly an improvement compared to the KdF-Wagen's 23-hp plant. The 985-cc flat-four came equipped with two carburetors, which is a common feature today on hopped-up air-cooled Volkswagens.

In a way, this is where the VW performance craze started . . . in 1939. Ferdinand Porsche conceived the groundbreaking Type 64/60K10 Berlin-Rome race car with Erwin Komenda overseeing the design and Karosserie Reutter the construction.

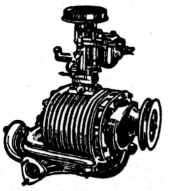

Only a little information is known about engineer Arno E.R. Koch's supercharger that was available as far back as 1951 in Germany. It seems to rely on the stock Solex 26-mm carburetor.

Moving ahead a few years, the situation looked rather grim in Germany immediately after the war's conclusion. Automobile racing slowly resumed before the turn of the decade, while car enthusiasts finally began having access to performance parts in the early 1950s. One of the most surprising setups appeared in an ad published in *Gute Fahrt* magazine in 1951, specifically a *Kompressor* (supercharger) promoted by Arno E.R. Koch from Frankfurt. Its commercial success apparently seemed limited.

Speaking of superchargers, other models became available during the second half of the 1950s. The biggest hit was the unit produced by Judson. The Conshohocken, Pennsylvania-based firm sold thousands, mostly for Volkswagens (with kits introduced in 1956) but also for Triumphs, MGs, and Renaults.

Judson conceived superchargers for a variety of automobiles, and thousands were sold as bolt-on kits for Volkswagens. This ad appeared in a 1966 issue of Foreign Car Guide, *and the system had been made for a decade by then.*

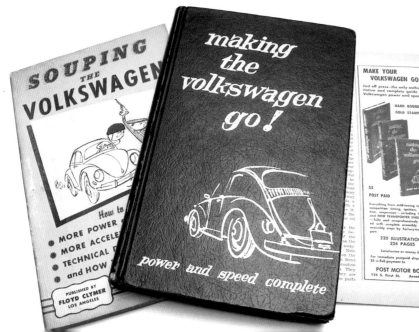

VW aficionados actively seek these two books that were first printed in the late 1950s/early 1960s: Souping the Volkswagen *and* Making the Volkswagen Go! *They confirm the interest generated by high-performance components at that time already. (Photo Courtesy Mike Walravens)*

As a side note, Judson made an electronic magneto as well. It is quite sought after by VW buffs today. Several other companies offered superchargers during the same era, including PEPCO (Ohio) and M.A.G. (Switzerland). They were joined in the mid-1960s by EMPI, and its setup manufactured by Shorrock (England).

The Search for Information

To get informed, folks interested in fast (make that fast*er*) Volkswagens relied first and foremost on the few magazine articles published at the time. A few books helped these gearheads in their quest for speed too: *Souping the Volkswagen* and *Making the Volkswagen Go!* published in the late 1950s and early 1960s, respectively. Both have become must-have items within the vintage VW performance scene along with Bill Fischer's *How to Hotrod Volkswagen Engines*, which was printed in 1970.

Today, as much as yesterday, one of the most popular add-ons within the same group remains the Okrasa kit. It was the work of engineer Gerhard Oettinger, the founder of Oettinger KRAftfahrtechnische Spezial-Anstalt (Oettinger Automobile Special Corporation), a.k.a. Okrasa, in 1951.

Oettinger's initial setup consisted in two Solex 32PBIC carburetors sitting atop bespoke manifolds, plus a pair of dual-port heads long before Volkswagen adopted them (1967). Customers could also select an optional chromoly crankshaft with a stroke of 64 mm (identical to stock) or 69.5 mm (the longer stroke led to a displacement of 1,300 cc instead of 1,200).

Okrasa products had quite a following in the United States as well. The company was helped by EMPI and other distributors, which started selling Herr Oettinger's kits in the 1950s. This proved the quality of the components, and even Volkswagen became interested. Volkswagen offered them as an option through the company's German dealers for a few months in 1963. The experience was short-lived as, apparently, VW head honcho Heinrich Nordhoff personally put a stop to these high-performance endeavors.

Okrasa expanded its line of products during the 1960s and 1970s. It remains very active in the tuner scene under the name Oettinger to this day. The company's old dual-carburetor/twin-port heads continue being beloved by enthusiasts, although the latter now have access to high-quality reproduction kits as well courtesy of Wolfsburg West in California.

Several other businesses tinkered with the VW powerplant through the 1950s, including coachbuilder Denzel from Austria. It supplied an array of high-quality components: heads and rocker arms, camshafts, counterweighted cranks, aluminum connecting rods and pistons, chromed aluminum cylinders, intake manifolds, and more. Few of these made it to the United States.

A superbly restored engine resides in Scott Tedro's 1951 Split Window sedan. It is the work of Buddy Hale and his crew at Type One Restorations in Arizona.

The 1,192-cc 40-hp motor (now bored to 1,385 cc) gained some gusto courtesy of a Judson supercharger. A bottle of Marvel Mystery Oil feeds its bearings.

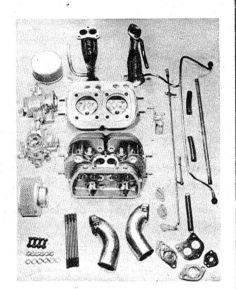
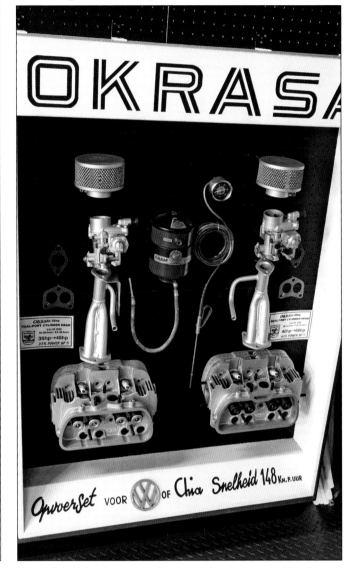

These quality pieces of speed equipment have been favorites with VW owners since 1951. Okrasa used dual Solex carburetors and trick dual-port heads 16 years before Volkswagen. (The Type 3 was the first model to receive dual-port heads.)

A cool display found in Japan's showroom at Flat4 promotes original Okrasa products in Dutch. With help from such kits, output jumped to 48 hp and 66 hp when mounted on 36-hp and the later 40-hp VW motors, respectively.

Curt Kolar installed a beautifully detailed 36-hp engine of 1959 vintage in his 1957 Oval Beetle. He added several interesting parts: a Porsche 356-style OT crank pulley and generator pulley, plus a Wolfsburg West Okrasa-style carburetor setup.

Austria's Wolfgang Denzel released high-tech engine kits during the 1950s, seen here in one of his own coachbuilt cars, the Denzel 1300. This example belongs to Mark Merrill. On the fan shroud is a Fram oil filter, which is popular with the vintage performance crowd.

Carburation Solutions

When it comes to carburation, numerous companies experimented with a wide assortment of models sourced in the United States or Europe during the 1960s. Scat Enterprises, which was founded in 1964 by Tom Lieb, released the Holley Bug-Spray single carburetor kit, an ex-Ford version available in 200-cfm or 300-cfm form.

Incidentally, Lieb went on to create a variety of other high-performance products through the 1960s. He was one of the very first to introduce counterweighted crankshafts in the U.S. VW industry as far back as 1966.

Yet again, EMPI aggressively marketed a range of carburetor kits. The 1964 catalog lists, among others, a single Zenith 30 mm on an EMPI manifold, along with a setup based on two 28-mm Solex carburetors (one of them was the stock unit; you simply had to purchase a second one plus a pair of manifolds). More EMPI offerings expanded the line as years passed, such as the twin Stromberg EMPI-Speedwell kit, twin Weber 38DCNLs, etc.

Some resourceful minds tinkered with models found on Porsches, most notably dual Zenith 32NDIXs and dual Solex 40 P11s. The latter equipped the first iteration

Henry Marchena's 1952 cabriolet runs a sought-after Autotechnic Express kit. It came with the following components: manifolds, the fuel filter, linkage, Knecht air filters, jets, and a second Solex 28PCI carburetor—the original was reused to complete the installation.

Ihr Volkswagen leistet noch mehr
durch die

2-VERGASER-EXPRESS-ANLAGE

AUTOTECHNIK KG
Hannover · Postfach 3030

Div. 2-Vergaser-Expreß-Anlagen auf Anfrage

This advertisement, which graced the pages of the German Gute Fahrt magazine in April 1955, shows the carburetor setup made by Autotechnik KG. It was one of the first dual-carburetor kits available on the market.

Here is a typical California Look VW engine from 1972 as found in Jim Edmiston's 1963 Bug that ran 13.20 seconds over the quarter mile. The 1,700-cc motor used a Bosch 010 distributor and Weber 48IDA carburetors that were set in motion by a Gene Berg linkage. (Photo Courtesy Jim Edmiston)

of EMPI's *Inch Pincher* drag Bug, as divulged in an article from *Hot Rod* magazine in August 1965, although they would soon be replaced with massive Weber 48IDAs.

The Mighty IDA

Within the air-cooled VW circles, the 48IDA enjoys cult status being used on the most powerful street and race cars. The Weber 46IDAs were found in racing Porsches in particular before gaining recognition in the United States when Caroll Shelby began using them on his almighty AC Cobra. The name of the first company that managed to make a pair of them work properly on a VW engine is a point of contention, although Scat Enterprises should be a strong contender.

Many more merchants made dual carburetor kits based on diverse models during the 1970s, such as DDS (Weber 40DCN), CB Performance (Weber IDF and later Dellorto), and others. Several outlets also supplied dual single-choke 40-mm Kadron/Solex carburetors, a Brazilian setup that emerged in 1972. It proves very popular to this day, especially on mild engines displacing under 2 liters.

Gene Berg Enterprises developed another kit that was highly regarded. It was based on two Weber 42DCNFs employed on fast 1970s Italian cars, particularly Maseratis. As an aside, the late Gene Berg (1936–1996) played a significant role in the VW performance industry. He started wrenching on Beetles in 1956, opened his first shop in Washington State in 1962, and then settled in California where he inaugurated Gene Berg Enterprises in 1969.

Berg's ingenuity led to the design of numerous pioneering parts during the 1960s and 1970s: oil sumps, higher-ratio rocker arms, heavier crankshaft pulleys, exhaust systems, etc. We also owe him for a sturdy dual carburetor linkage that bolts to the VW engine's fan shroud. Originated

With the old PEPCO's blower being in short supply, Ray Schubert at Speedwell USA stepped up and made an exact copy with improved internals for 25/36-hp VW flat-fours (1949-1960). Such setup equips Pip Hancox's rare 1949 Beetle. A Solex 30PICT (topped by a bespoke K&N-based air filter) supplies the air and fuel.

Most accessories unveiled in the chapter cater to the performance crowd. This one? Not so much . . . It fits under the engine's sump plate to warm up the oil in regions where Volkswagens face harsh winter conditions.

This frame shows a range of advertisement for EMPI products, including the "exciting new sound of the 1970s" for the company's latest range of exhaust systems.

The Volkswagen aftermarket exploded during the 1960s, and numerous firms mainly involved in domestic automobiles jumped on the bandwagon. Among them was Weiand, which casted this attractive engine pulley cover.

in 1965, it has received a variety of small improvements through the decades, making it a VW enthusiast's favorite to this day. Other companies came up with other cross-bar-style linkages, such as EMPI and Tayco.

Breathe Out

When installing one of the above carburetor setups, VW buffs typically changed the exhaust system as well to let the motor "breathe" properly. Abarth from Italy tapped that market as early as the 1950s, offering products for varied European automobiles. The model that was conceived for Volkswagens (characterized by the four tips protruding from the muffler) sold in great numbers in many countries starting with the United States.

Still on the subject of exhaust systems, VW enthusiasts had access to better-designed headers featuring equal-length tubing in the 1960s and 1970s. Among them were EMPI, DDS, Fourtuned, Gene Berg, S&S, and Cyclone. They were occasionally paired with not-so-efficient mufflers filled with a sound-absorbing material (a.k.a. "glasspack mufflers"). They are difficult

to locate today, as they rarely stood the test of time.

With the Manx-style dune buggy craze going full swing throughout the 1960s and 1970s, some engine-specific add-ons appeared on the market. They included exhaust headers and mufflers along with pulley guards of various shapes and forms. One of the rarest is the version made by Weiand, which is a name more often associated with the V-8 performance world.

Ignition Options

Ignition was another area of interest for the young tuners at the time. They discovered that the Bosch 010 used on 1959 and 1960 VW Buses offered an efficient advance curve, which is why these units continue to be hunted down by collectors today. Finding one in good shape can be difficult, but they look great with their small identification tab riveted on their body. Suppliers better known in the V-8 world later released their own distributor as well; Mr. Gasket and Mallory come to mind.

One of the most impressive ignition setups remains the magneto, which produces a high-energy spark. First adopted by VW drag racers, they made their way to the street. The Scintilla Vertex was a favorite. Specialists such as Joe Hunt and Don Zig continue the legacy of servicing

and selling magnetos today.

While some may argue magnetos aren't as efficient as modern ignitions, they have "that look." Just make sure to support the unit with a bracket due to its heavy weight. It could otherwise damage the engine case over time.

Locating any of the above-mentioned components often translates into a challenge due to their use/abuse and an occasional lack of spare parts for the most complex pieces. However, some enthusiasts have truly embraced these vintage high-performance goodies, thus creating "sporty" Bugs that solely include era-correct parts.

The trend, known as Old Speed within the VW scene, often involved early models (Split and Oval Windows). However, it is not limited to engines, as players also seek other 1950s and early-1960s race-oriented items from early Porsche 356 rims to aftermarket gauges. All are great ways to personalize a Volkswagen while managing to easily and confidently zip through today's frenzied traffic. A complete chapter is devoted to the Old Speed subject later in this book.

Fitted in a 1967 Cal Look Bug, Rick Sadler's monster 227-hp 2,387-cc engine uses a pair of Italian-made Weber 48IDAs carburetors and a Joe Hunt Vertex magneto, which is supported by a sturdy aluminum bracket.

Dave Galassi's 1962 Beetle Sedan

Dave Galassi found inspiration in the original V-8 gassers when building his high-performance Beetle, solely using parts manufactured during the 1960s.

While the style of this Beetle may puzzle some readers, it makes sense from a historical perspective. It takes its inspiration from V-8 drag cars that were immensely popular during the 1960s: the Gassers, which packed a ton of horsepower and often featured a nose-high stance. The National Hot Rod Association (NHRA) even had classes for them, and Volkswagen occasionally joined them, some with great success in H/Gas and I/Gas. EMPI's *Inch Pincher* Bug remains the most recognized of the bunch.

To illustrate this V-8 and VW connection, I photographed Dave Galassi's 1962 Beetle in the company of his friend Dale Snoke's 10-second street/strip 1964 Mercury Comet, which is one of the most recognized (contemporary) examples of the genre. The pictures will divulge various traits they have in common, including the hand-laid gold-leaf lettering and the suspension set high, although the L87 Pearl White VW ragtop simply retains its factory height.

Galassi grew up in Pasadena, a Southern Californian city with deep historical ties to the hot rod world. One of the local outlets, Blair's Speed Shop, built an impressive number of Gassers during the 1960s, and he used to visit the place as a kid. He also admired the VW Gasser scene's pioneers, who did marvels creating innovative cars at a time when few high-performance parts existed. This led to the *Davey and Goliath* project, based on the idea of a Gasser someone might have built around 1966, before Volkswagen released its dual-port heads.

Work began on the well-preserved, 92,000-mile 1962 Bug that Galassi purchased from the original owner in the 1990s. Several hard-to-find components, such as the supercharger, came from friend George Schmidt. PEPCO manufactured the unit, and it apparently flows better than the renowned Judson blower.

The 1585-cc engine assembled by Schmidt employs single-port heads, along with (almost) only parts from the 1960s. The parts include a Gene Berg 69-mm crank, a Cyclone header, and a Racetrim oil sump. The crank pulleys are welded together; one of them spins the supercharger at a higher speed than PEPCO's setup to increase boost. It took days to properly tune the carburetor, a 45-mm Weber DCOE modified by Augie Delgado with one barrel machined off. The engine delivers 100 hp, a commendable figure considering the small displacement.

Galassi collects rare magnesium VW rims, hence he dug in his stash of BRMs and American Racing Torq-Thrusts. He settled on a beautiful set of the latter in 15x5 with new old stock (NOS) center caps. They run 215/65-15 M&H Racemaster cheater slicks in the back.

A company specializing in aircraft windshields made the fantastic decklid inspired by the outlandish 1960s custom show cars, in addition to the acrylic lenses that cover the NOS motorcycle headlights (a nod to the 1960s and 1970s VW drag racers who chose them for their light weight). The lack of bumpers and painted logos on the body by artist Larry Fator contribute to the Gasser vibe. Finally, the fully redone cockpit houses a handful of desirable components, including a Superior 500 steering wheel and an old Iskenderian clip on the dash.

Galassi's well-accessorized Beetle is always certain to please the crowd, either at car shows or drag strips. He incidentally lives close to Southern California's Irwindale Raceway. An unusual time machine, his ride beautifully celebrates the Gasser heroes of yesteryear.

These are two very cool Gassers with different powerplants. Secured with three quick-release pins, the clear decklid features an opening for the carburetor's velocity stack.

While it never achieved the same commercial success as the Judson supercharger, PEPCO's well-built unit remains highly regarded within the vintage VW crowd. Notice the use of an original Bosch 010 distributor.

After unsuccessfully trying an old carburetor from a 1965 Chevy Corvair Turbo, Dave Galassi and friend George Schmidt settled on a heavily modified Weber DCOE carb. The plate riveted on the side of the supercharger lists a "Date of Overhaul" of May 23, 1961.

Performance-oriented goodies include a Superior 500 steering wheel and a Sun tachometer, which are both period-correct of course. This rather uncommon piece was made to work on 4-cylinder engines only.

The NHRA's Gas class rules mandated headlights back in the day. However, some resourceful racers changed over to lighter units. In the case of Dave Galassi's ragtop, they hide behind tinted acrylic covers.

CHAPTER 7

WHEELS: ROLLING DOWN THE ROAD IN STYLE

As anyone who has visited Volkswagen shows may attest, wheels remain one of the most popular ways to personalize a Beetle—or any other member from the air-cooled VW family for that matter.

Today's enthusiast can choose between dozens of new models ready to bolt on, which can easily be purchased online or via local Volkswagen shops. Yet, there is a fringe group of fanatics that would rather find decades-old rims for their rides, especially individuals who have already spent a ton of energy, let alone green bills, finding other rare accessories for their project cars.

The number of wheels specifically designed for air-cooled Volkswagens since the 1960s is truly astounding. Showing all of them in this chapter is impossible, but the following paragraphs list a large chunk of them, thereby hopefully helping some restorers in a quest for those elusive pieces.

Start Measuring

Defining if a wheel fits a specific car should be the first item on any restorer's agenda. Thankfully, Volkswagen did not make countless changes when it comes

Denny Aker's 1963 Beetle hasn't changed since he built it in the 1960s. The conversion involved a bunch of Porsche 356 parts: chrome wheels, aluminum brakes, and one of the sports car world's most desirable engines: a 1959 four-cam 1588-cc Carrera flat-four!

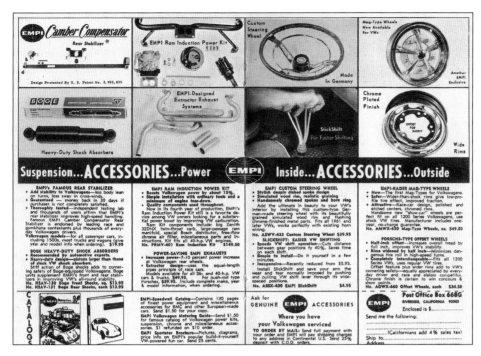

bolt pattern. The same applies when browsing the alleys of a swap meet, where a tape measure will be a friend.

See those interesting old steel wheels with a wide-five bolt pattern? Well, they could be for a British-made Ford Anglia (better known as Ford Popular in the UK). The bolt pattern happens to be oh-so-slightly different from the 5x205-mm layout we all know, as England didn't use the metric system.

Also, don't get too excited when discovering some four-lug rims that you swear you've seen on a Beetle before. They might fit a Datsun or a Ford Pinto for instance, but they definitely won't bolt right on 4x130-mm VW drums or discs.

During the search for the perfect wheels, double-check the overall diameter as well. Most Bug versions measure 15 inches, except Split Windows produced prior to October 1952, which ran 16s. Sure, the VW scene has embraced large-diameter wheels in recent years, but 15s remain the most popular choice to this day, especially on cars retaining their vintage character. Numerous old, aftermarket rims come in 13 or 14 inches too, but check to see if they will properly fill the wheel wells.

During the 2006 VW Classic show, Der Kleiner Panzers club celebrated the 50-year anniversary of the magnesium BRM and American Racing VW wheels. The group managed to gather 58 BRM wheels (with 28 of them on cars) and 20 American Racing wheels. Their added value was more than $175,000.

Also keep in mind that a rare and obscure wheel does not make it necessarily desirable. A manufacturer might have produced only a small batch of a certain model because it never achieved commercial success. To be blunt, enthusiasts could have considered it pretty ugly back then. Tastes occasionally change over time, and these old dogs may suddenly be in high demand but not always. There will be plenty of not-so-pretty and cheaply made wheels for sale at VW shows. Then again, beauty is in the eye of the beholder as they say, right?

to the bolt pattern. In the United States, Bugs retained 5x205-mm (a.k.a. "wide five") rims through 1967. This was replaced with 4x130-mm versions that were used until the end of the car's production in Mexico in 2003. (As a side note, certain VW Buses came with a 5x112-mm bolt pattern starting in 1971 depending on the markets.)

So, before getting excited about some apparently rare rims found via an internet ad, ask the seller about the

The Year Was 1962

Car enthusiasts had limited choices when it came to wheels after the war and through the 1950s. America's custom car scene, which was dominated by V-8 automobiles, made do with chromed versions, occasionally featuring different offsets. VW owners, on the other hand, occasionally personalized their rides with slotted Porsche 15-inch wheels that were used on post-1955 356s. They bolted right on the VWs' 5x205-mm drums. They looked great but proved expensive, hence some folks made do with 356 hubcaps only or no hubcaps at all to mimic the Porsche race cars.

The tide began to turn in 1962–1963, when a few companies started producing custom wheels in larger quantities. One of the most successful was the five-spoke

Leroy Wright still belongs to the Volks Chancellors, a Los Angeles–based club established in 1965. In the early 1970s, he drove this late-model Bug running Cragar rims. Notice the four-lug VW pattern (front) and five-lug "domestic" pattern (back), the latter requiring adapters. (Photo Courtesy Volks Chancellors)

Canada's Ken King has been known to save even the crustiest VW Buses, including this very rare 1953 23-window Deluxe Microbus that is fitted with vintage 15x6 Calparts wheels.

Cragar's Super Sport (S/S) model introduced in 1964 for domestic automobiles. It incorporated five steel locking clips into the aluminum spokes, making it stronger and safer than most OEM and aftermarket offerings at the time. Cragar went on to equip a wide range of vehicles during the 1960s and 1970s from dune buggies and vans to street machines and drag cars.

The V-8 world embraced the S/S, but there was a catch for VW owners. They featured the wrong offset and bolt pattern, so wheel adapters were needed. The result wasn't always pretty, as rims and tires often protruded from the fenders.

Eventually, several companies began manufacturing custom wheels specifically for Volkswagens with

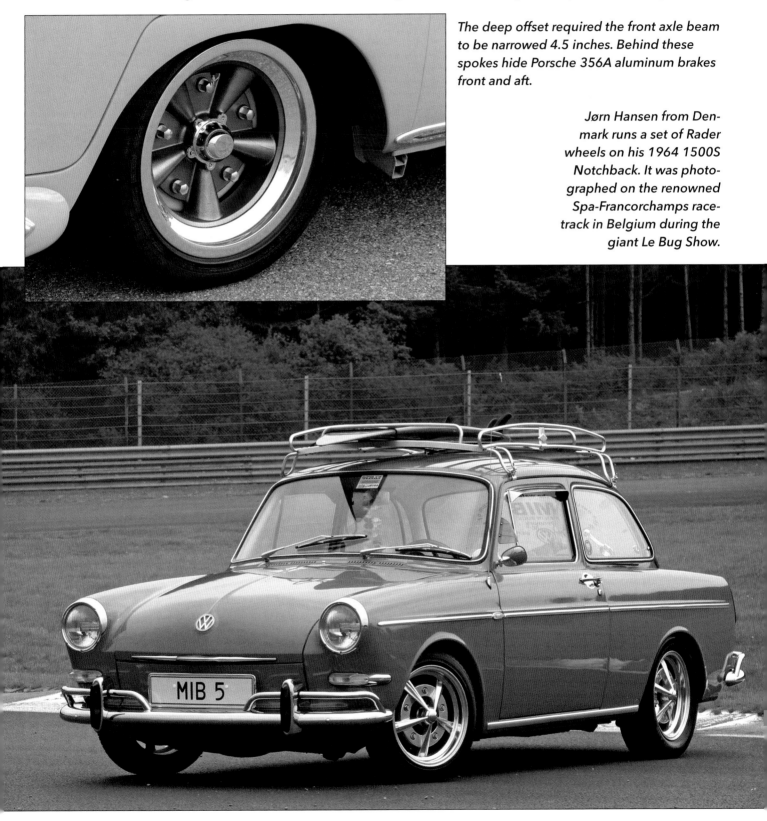

The deep offset required the front axle beam to be narrowed 4.5 inches. Behind these spokes hide Porsche 356A aluminum brakes front and aft.

Jørn Hansen from Denmark runs a set of Rader wheels on his 1964 1500S Notchback. It was photographed on the renowned Spa-Francorchamps racetrack in Belgium during the giant Le Bug Show.

American readers might recognize this wheel as the EMPI Sprint Star. However, it was actually manufactured in Germany by Lemmerz. In 1966, the price was 36 Deutschmarks ($9.07) for the painted version and 96 ($24.18) for the chromed.

EMPI Sprint Stars fit nicely under factory VW fenders, as is demonstrated by John Rayburn's 1964 sedan (bought new by his parents). Measuring 15x4.5 and 15x5.5, they respectively run Vredestein 155/70 and meaty BFGoodrich 235/60 tires.

the correct 5x205-mm bolt pattern. This included the five-spoke models from E-T, Calparts, Crestline, and Rocket, although their offset was often better suited for dune buggies than Beetles.

One of the best fits remained the Räder (occasionally spelled Rader) rim, launched by entrepreneur Dick Rader, as seen on the EMPI *Inch Pincher* drag car in 1965. As an interesting aside, the word *Räder* means "wheel" in German. They came in two versions: with the spokes being either flat or topped with a single rib. They soon experienced some success; even the Sears Roebuck chain of stores carried them. EMPI sold these wheels as well, hav-ing them listed in its 1966 catalog together with other five-lug rims, such as the EMPI Sprint Star and the five-spoke EMPI GT.

Along Came the BRM

Another model unveiled in the same 1966 EMPI catalog piqued the interest of the high-performance folks in particular: the magnesium BRM. Its development came thanks to a venture between EMPI and Speedwell, a motorsport-oriented company based in England. It was run in part by Graham Hill, best known for his success as a Formula 1 racer. He had joined the BRM F1 team in 1960.

While stock VW rims measured 15x4 starting in October 1952, the new BRMs added 1 inch in width and proved very light, tipping the scale at 7.5 pounds. The rims gained national attention when they appeared on the EMPI *Inch Pincher* drag racing Bug, which graced the cover of *Rod & Custom* magazine in October 1966.

Their magnesium construction had some drawbacks. It made them prone to corrosion, and the spokes were fragile and known to crack. The same issue occasionally affected the two-piece cast-aluminum EMPI GT. BRM wheels are still sought after today with sets of four often changing hands for more than $10,000.

From Washington state, Marc Buehler's red 1951 Bug remains almost unchanged since it appeared in the February 1975 issue of hotVWs *magazine. It even retains its original BRM wheels with Michelin tires purchased new in 1978.*

NEW FROM EMPI and a VW owners delight, is this lightweight mag safety wheel for beetles at $49.50 ea. Write: EMPI, Dept. RC10, P.O. Box 668, Riverside, Calif., for full details on these BRM made beauties.

The October 1966 issue of Rod & Custom *magazine introduced the new BRM "mag" (short for magnesium), sold by EMPI in the United States and Speedwell in the United Kingdom. The 7.5-pound rim cost $49.50 that year.*

Other magnesium rims hit the market at the same time. Hot rod fans are likely familiar with the name American Racing Equipment (ARE), a company founded in 1956. ARE began making a beautiful five-spoke magnesium wheel in 1963, and a very desirable model known as Torq-Thrust is still available today in aluminum.

Three years later, the manufacturer released a five-spoke with an identical design and 5x205-mm bolt-pattern for the VW crowd. Through the 1960s and 1970s, ARE designed a number of magnesium and aluminum rims for the VW market featuring the 5x205-mm bolt pattern (La Paz model), 4x130 mm (Silverstone, Le Mans), as well as 5x130 mm used on Porsches. We'll get to the Porsche subject in a minute.

Spokes 'n Slots

During the second half of the 1960s, more companies took interest in Volkswagens with two-piece fabrication being common. Names include Chaparral, Big Wheels, and the flat-spoked Walker. The 1966 Astro catalog shows a neat five-spoke version known as the Continental, which is hard to find today like many of the aforementioned models.

Unveiled in Chapter 6, Dave Galassi's supercharged 1962 Bug rolls on a set of American Racing Torq-Thrust mags, a rare 15x5 model with VW bolt pattern (note the NOS center caps). Rear tires are 215/65-15 M&H Racemaster cheater slicks. The four drums were converted from bolts to studs, which is a common practice to this day in the air-cooled Volkswagen scene.

Bob Allen's 1969 Beetle ran slot (Shelby-style) rims, a spoiler, and a wild paint job. Ansen was one of the first companies to produce this type of wheel.

So-called slot rims offered by manufacturers such as Ansen had a strong following as well. Their design incorporated large openings/slots (typically five) on their face, along with the 5x205-mm bolt pattern, which was later followed by the 4x130.

Deano Dyno Soars (DDS), a purveyor of high-performance VW parts since 1968, unveiled one of the most basic yet unusual wheels during the late 1960s. Its three-piece construction imagined

Paul Schley (pictured) and his brother Mark campaigned the legendary Lightning Bug 2, *the very first Volkswagen sedan to cover the quarter mile in less than 11 seconds (1972).*

by brothers Ken and Dean Lowry called for a center made of a flat sheet of aluminum. The goal was to create one of the lightest rims available for drag racing. Offered with a 13- or 15-inch diameter, several sets came to be used on the street, although they proved rather fragile.

While many VW fanatics dreamed of owning magnesium or aluminum wheels, budget often dictated the purchase of more affordable steel counterparts. Rocket had a variety of them available through its 1968 catalog a few years before Mangels from Brazil flooded the U.S. market with entry-level wheels of different styles. Fans

of off-road competition might remember the name Jackman as well, which produced a range of five- and four-lug rims, used in competitions, such as Mexico's Baja 1000.

More from the 1970s

Enthusiasts had access to an increasing number of new wheels through the 1970s in both early 5x205-mm and late 4x130-mm bolt patterns. Volkswagen of America had an interesting offering via its Formula Vee line mentioned in Chapter 2: the four-lug,

The Schley duo selected lightweight 13- and 15-inch DDS rims that weigh 3.9 pounds and 5.4 pounds, respectively. Amazingly, the chopped 1960 Volkswagen tipped the scale at only 1,064 pounds.

Jackman produced basic steel wheels that were popular with the off-road community. The same company also made a lesser-known riveted version featuring the same design but in aluminum, as is seen on Bud Bulmer's 1967 Beetle. They measure 15x4 and 15x6.5.

VW drag racers and off-roaders have adopted Centerline rims since the mid-1970s before they hit the street. Built in the spirit of that era, Jean-Louis "Frenchy" Dehoux's California Look 1954 Bug uses 15x4s and 15x5.5s.

was replaced by a slotted rim nicknamed Turtleback that was produced by Superior Industries in 1972.

Still in the same 4x130-mm category was EMPI's two-piece eight-spoke GT that became a popular choice, eclipsing lesser-known models manufactured by Keystone and others. Both Appliance and Durachrome made several four-lug wheels too, although they had already marketed five-lug products prior to them.

During the mid-1970s, a riveted aluminum five-lug version created by Centerline turned into a hit with off-road and drag racers. But once again, owners of custom Volkswagens took a liking to them. They soon trickled down onto the street as well. Centerline offered a wide range of sizes, including 13x5.5s introduced in 1976.

With Volkswagens flooding the roads of America through the 1970s, local wheel manufacturers went to great lengths to get a piece of that thriving market. However, the rest of the world did not sit idle, releasing their share of new products. Enthusiasts in

five-spoke GT Mag (not to be confused with EMPI's version) is better known as Riviera today. The GT Mag was "made of a special aluminum-magnesium-beryllium-titanium alloy" according to VW's catalog. It

While some folks may confuse these wheels for EMPI Sprint Stars, they happen to be South African Rostyles. They dress Ken King's 1954 Kombi, which was delivered new in Canada with a sunroof option.

It is a safe bet that few readers have caught sight of such wheels on U.S. roads. Called Fumagalli, they came all the way from Brazil and equip Alan Meier's mega-detailed 1957 cabriolet.

South Africa, where Beetles sold very well, had access to the Rostyle, which had a peculiar offering of a wide-five version. (Bugs still used 5x205-mm drums in that country during the 1970s.) Available via VW dealerships, it resembles EMPI's Sprint Star.

In Australia, VW owners had access to a rim called the Flower. Brazil produced various uniquely designed models, such as the five-lug Fumagalli and Titanio Venus.

As one might expect, Germany got into the game as well with the five- and four-lug Remotec, the Ronal Kleeblatt, and others. In France, Delta Mics manufactured sporty-looking five-lug alloys. The Cosmic name enjoyed some success in the UK too. This aluminum rim was available for numerous European cars during the 1970s: post-1967 Volkswagens (15x5.5 and 15x6), Porsche 911s (15x5.5), etc.

The Porsche Connection

Speaking of Porsches, the 356 wasn't the only vehicle to inspire VW buffs. The release of the Porsche 914 (VW-Porsche 914 in Europe) allowed access to new

Spotted in action during the DAS Drag Day in Germany is a local Split Window Bug wearing a set of Remotec rims. The Remotec model was available in a variety of bolt patterns: 5x205-mm VW, 4x130-mm VW, and 5x130-mm Porsche.

Cosmic offered its alloys with multiple bolt patterns, offsets, and sizes. As a general rule, check all measurements before spending hard-earned cash on potentially collectible wheels.

Here is more action from DAS Drag Day. Visiting European events allows gearheads to discover unusual rims, such as 15x5.5 Porsche 914-style Pedrinis (beige Bug) and 14x5.5 Hegglins (green Bug).

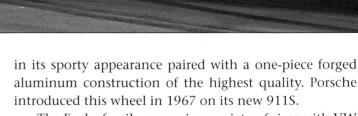

high-quality wheels through either Porsche or VW dealerships depending on the country. Available from 1969 until 1976, the mid-engine two-seater used mostly VW Type 4 motors, as found on 411s, 412s, and some 1972-and-later Type 2s. These flat-fours displaced 1.7, 1.8, or 2.0 liters, although a small number of 914s (known as 914/6s) ran a 2.0-litre Porsche flat-six.

The 4-cylinder 914 came with a variety of 4x130-mm rims, starting with simple steel versions made by Lemmerz or Kronprinz. (Incidentally, both manufactured other aftermarket VW wheels). They were complemented by fancy-looking 4x130-mm alloys from Fuchs with a four-spoke clover design, Pedrini, or Mahle (nicknamed Baby Gasburner within the VW hobby).

The 914/6 came standard with 5x130-mm steel rims. There were two 5x130-mm options available through the years: Fuchs or Mahle with a flatter design (and lighter weight thanks to the use of magnesium). These models, which came on Porsche 911s as well, will not fit Volkswagens without some alterations.

As an aside, the vintage 5x130-mm Fuchs alloy has a special place in many VW enthusiasts' hearts. It has been a favorite since the mid-1970s, when it became an integral part of the California Look. Some of its appeal lies in its sporty appearance paired with a one-piece forged aluminum construction of the highest quality. Porsche introduced this wheel in 1967 on its new 911S.

The Fuchs family comes in a variety of sizes with VW fans often selecting hard-to-find 15x4.5s or 15x5.5s for the front that are complemented with 15x6s for the rear. Again, check the markings on the back of the wheels when looking for a set at a swap meet, as some measure 14 inches (1960s) and others 16 (starting in 1977).

Using adapters will not work best in most cases, as this route will translate into a wider track, meaning that the tires might stick out from the fenders, especially in the front. A better solution involves redrilling the factory 4x130-mm VW drums (or discs) into Porsche's 5x130-mm bolt pattern, which is a straightforward task with the right tools. In recent years, various companies have also

Very popular in the air-cooled Volkswagen world, Porsche's Fuchs wheels come in various sizes. The 15x4.5 and 15x6 from the 1960s are favorites, as are found on Casey Viscioni's street-and-strip 1962 Beetle.

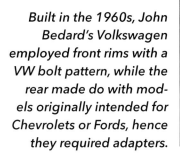

Built in the 1960s, John Bedard's Volkswagen employed front rims with a VW bolt pattern, while the rear made do with models originally intended for Chevrolets or Fords, hence they required adapters.

been selling brake kits already set up with the Porsche bolt pattern that are ready to install on any air-cooled Volkswagen.

Make Them Fit

If the truth be told, most any vintage wheel can be made to fit under the fenders of a Beetle with some engineering. For example, customizers occasionally resort to narrowing the front axle beam or shortening the rear axles. Add redrilled drums and/or discs in the correct bolt pattern, or complete made-to-fit brake kits, and you're in business.

How about tires? Unfortunately, their rubber compounds deteriorate with time and certainly don't age as well as aluminum or steel. Poor storage, exposure to sunlight, and a damp climate affects their lifetime too. Think twice before installing these good-looking (but hard-as-rocks) NOS Goodyear Blue Streak tires from the 1960s. Thankfully, the aftermarket industry has plenty to offer with companies such as Coker duplicating a lot of

the old rubber. No one will feel offended if you use accurate reproductions of Firestone, Goodyear, Michelin, or Pirelli tires of yesteryear.

There are still so many wheels to be discovered. Check out the rare and beautifully detailed 15x4.5 ICMP alloys found on Paul Davis's 1963 Type 3 Squareback.

CHAPTER 8

TRAVELING: HAPPILY HITTING THE STREET

Holiday travel in America has undoubtedly changed since the 1950s and 1960s. We all take plane trips for granted today, but only the wealthiest could afford a ticket back then. The experience was quite different too, as the happy few wore fine clothes and enjoyed fancy meals that were followed, of course, by a cigarette.

Most everyone therefore journeyed by car, often using new roads since the government had expanded highway projects after World War II. Countless people did so in a Beetle. Many have been driven coast to coast, although they aren't the roomiest, and crossing the desert in the summer certainly wasn't the most pleasant experience.

Indeed, VW buyers occasionally chose the dealer-installed air-conditioning system that was offered as an option by U.S. VW dealers starting in 1967. However, it had drawbacks, being bulky (it made engine maintenance more challenging) and marginally efficient compared to 21st-century installations. Customers often complained about the fact that it "stole horsepower" and, worse, sometimes led to overheating the engine.

Geared toward the travelers, this spread found in a 1968 VW catalog shows several accessories available through dealerships—most importantly a trailer hitch and a roof rack.

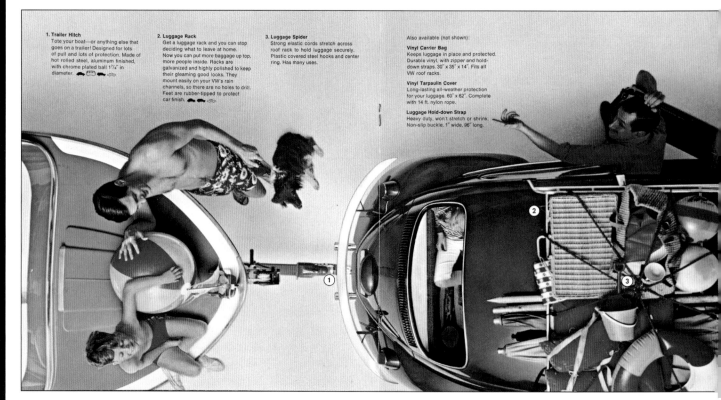

1. Trailer Hitch
Tote your boat—or anything else that goes on a trailer! Designed for lots of pull and lots of protection. Made of hot rolled steel, aluminum finished, with chrome plated ball 1⁷/₈" in diameter.

2. Luggage Rack
Get a luggage rack and you can stop deciding what to leave at home. Now you can put more baggage up top, more people inside. Racks are galvanized and highly polished to keep their gleaming good looks. They mount easily on your VW's rain channels, so there are no holes to drill. Feet are rubber-tipped to protect car finish.

3. Luggage Spider
Strong elastic cords stretch across roof rack to hold luggage securely. Plastic covered steel hooks and center ring. Has many uses.

Also available (not shown):

Vinyl Carrier Bag
Keeps luggage in place and protected. Durable vinyl, with zipper and hold-down straps. 30" x 35" x 14". Fits all VW roof racks.

Vinyl Tarpaulin Cover
Long-lasting all-weather protection for your luggage. 60" x 62". Complete with 14 ft. nylon rope.

Luggage Hold-down Strap
Heavy duty, won't stretch or shrink. Non-slip buckle. 1" wide, 96" long.

Nicknamed the poor man's air conditioner, car coolers, such as this Cool-O-Matic example, contain a water reservoir, which evaporates as the vehicle is in motion, creating refreshing moisture.

From Hot to Cold

On the other hand, traveling in colder areas required efficient heating. Volkswagen's setup relied on heat generated from the exhaust system, which worked marginally well in very cold climates. The German manufacturer therefore supplied optional devices that mounted under the hood (on the side of the front trunk) on most models or in the engine compartment in the case of Buses.

It may come as a surprise: This apparatus runs on gasoline drawn from the fuel tank but remains a safe alternative to this day if in good condition and properly maintained.

How does it work? On most VW systems, gasoline is delivered to the heater from the fuel tank. Then, a fan blows air into a combustion chamber where a glow plug lights the air/fuel mixture. Ducting around the chamber contains a second fan, which blows air warmed by contact with the combustion chamber before reaching the cockpit. Don't worry, spent gasses are obviously routed outside the vehicle.

Most units found in old Volkswagens worldwide were made by Eberspächer and apparently installed by either VW dealers when cars arrived at their destination or directly at the VW factories. In the United States, Stewart-Warner supplied dealerships with its own South Wind kit, which was approved to be used as an option by Volkswagen. The aftermarket also offered different gas-powered systems, such as the model manufactured by Webasto, a company known for its Beetle sunroofs too.

So, let's pretend you're planning a summer vacation trip or a shorter getaway. Do you have your checklist in hand? On Beetles, baggage could fit in the small cubby hole behind the rear seat or under the hood, although space proved rather limited. Several companies thereby made pieces of luggage specifically designed to take advantage of every cubic inch in the trunk.

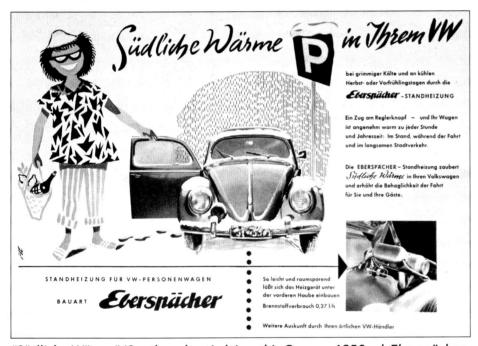

"Südliche Wärme" (Southern heat) claims this German 1958 ad. Eberspächer gas heaters are indeed quite efficient in very cold weather. The company later supplied Volkswagen with almost identical kits for the VW Thing.

To keep cool during long journeys, some people on a tighter budget installed a car cooler (better known as swamp cooler) on the passenger-side door. This evaporative air cooler typically took the shape of a round canister that contained a water reservoir with a pad. It worked as follows: With the vehicle in forward motion, air was forced into the tube. Water inside the unit would then evaporate, thus creating moisture-laden air that would reach the car's interior through vents. The passenger-side window would have to remain slightly open. The system would be quite efficient in low-humidity regions, providing relief from the heat for 100 to 150 miles.

If you still ran out of space, getting a roof rack was the next step. Just make sure to mount it properly with rubber pads to avoid damaging the rain gutters. Some racks even fit in the back of the vehicle bolted to the bumper. To keep their belongings dry while journeying, VW owners occasionally installed an enclosed box on the roof rather than a rack, including the model from

Rare Vintage Air VW Club President Frank Espinoza owns a 1950 Split Window Bug fitted with an unusual divider. It made the interior quieter and more difficult for thieves to access in case they wanted to steal luggage behind the rear seat.

"Would you like to bring some luggage for four people during your next trip?" asked Richter & Co. In 1953, it offered this solution: a suitcase purposely shaped to reside behind a Beetle's fuel tank.

Rather than resting in and putting strain on the rain gutters, Heinrich Eckel's roof rack advertised in 1957 used four suction cups. Its design allowed the unit to be mounted on non-VW cars too.

Not all luggage racks fit on the roof, as was demonstrated by the chromed version marketed by Fenestra-Crittall in 1955. With such an option, occupants could still enjoy the Volkswagen's sunroof.

In case Beetle owners were afraid someone would snag their belongings from the roof rack, Audaco conceived an enclosed model that nicely follows the car's roof lines. The advertisement dates back to 1954.

The "Frühstücktischchen" (small breakfast table) cleverly slid over the glove-box door. This 1957 advertisement shows the dash of an Oval Window Bug, which was a model built from 1953 until 1957.

Audaco, which neatly followed the shape of a Beetle's top.

As you might expect, Volkswagen offered its share of travel-friendly items that were available through its dealer network. A few of these goodies appeared in its 1968 catalog. It introduced the new Bug, which was characterized by its bulkier bumpers. The list included a trailer hitch that was ideal to tow a small boat along with a luggage rack and luggage spider, which was a welcome addition to avoid flyaway cargo when in motion. The brochure listed but did not show a few other items to be used with the roof rack: a 30x35x14-inch vinyl carrier bag, a 60x62-inch vinyl tarpaulin cover, and luggage hold-down straps.

A Table and a Coffee

Time to move inside the cockpit. With GPS being decades away, maps were obviously a must. You can find plenty of 1950s/1960s examples in antique stores. A radio proved to be a welcome addition when cruising on long and occasionally boring stretches of highway.

Family travels often involved picnicking. Several surprising accessories made the experience more enjoyable, including the Frühstückstischchen (small breakfast table) advertised in *Gute Fahrt* magazine in 1957. It affixed to the Beetle's opened glove-box door.

In Germany, Paluxette also supplied a coffee machine, which plugged into the socket that was intended for the cigarette lighter. (Incidentally, the latter was a popular option installed by Volkswagen dealers for years.) Brewing a cup of joe on the move was definitely not the best idea, as both the outside of the maker and, obviously, its contents got seriously hot. While Paluxette's machines were compact in size, other

Kaffee am Steuer

Mit unverminderter Geschwindigkeit weiterfahren, keinen Augenblick die Fahrbahn aus den Augen lassen und trotzdem dabei eine Tasse Kaffee kochen, - das klingt fast unglaublich, - wird aber zur Tatsache durch unsere

Autokaffeemaschine

PALUXETTE

Ohne Mitführung von Kaffeegeschirr durch einfaches Auswechseln von fertig gefüllten Kaffeekapseln, erhalten Sie mühelos einen duftenden, köstlichen Filterkaffee. Darauf wurde bei der Konstruktion besonderer Wert gelegt.

Gegen **Übermüdung** am Steuer, **Erfrischung** zu jeder Zeit, der letzte u. **nützlichste** Komfort für Ihr Auto.

Lassen Sie sich diese Neuheit von Ihrem Autohändler vorführen.

Hersteller: **Fa. Patzner K. G. Bad Mergentheim**

Who needs to swing by Starbucks when you have a Paluxette automatic coffee machine in your Volkswagen? It plugs into the cigarette lighter. Just make sure not to turn it on while driving.

brands made larger units through the years that were better adapted to VW campers, such as Westfalias.

The concept of automotive safety has undoubtedly evolved since the 1950s. In fact, seat belts only became mandatory equipment on all cars when the 1968 models were introduced in the United States. Through the 1970s, mom and dad never thought twice about letting their kids roam freely in the back of their Beetle.

Scottish actor Ewan McGregor, a fan of air-cooled Volkswagens who is better known for his role in the Star Wars saga, concurs. He remembered traveling as a young kid in his family's Bug during the mid-1970s: "When going on summer vacation to France for instance, my parents would make the back of the car flat, so that my brother and I would have a place to sleep at night. We were already dressed in pajamas. I think my love for Beetles comes from these trips."

If the truth be told, folding the rear seat made the rear area somewhat flat. Although, VW owners had other options, including the Wagendeck that was advertised in *Foreign Car Guide* in 1963. It called for folding the rear bench seat with trick brackets, thus improving loading capacity. It was perfect for transporting boxes or, well, children.

Seen in a circa 1956-1957 sedan, a Paluxette coffee maker is in good company. The vehicle also had a Motorola radio, VDO clock, locking steering column, Banjo steering wheel, and grab handle. The old canister contains replacement bulbs.

This is the NEW WAGENDECK

CAR·CRAFTERS COMPANY

WAGENDECK makes your VW a station wagon

Wagendeck gives you 12 square feet of flat storage space in your VW. Plenty of space to carry groceries, luggage, camping equipment, golf clubs, merchandise, books, children.

No alterations necessary. Installs in minutes. A pair of hinge arms and angle brackets supplied with the kit allow you to flip the back seat forward and out of the way—

no need to remove the seat cushion!

The Wagendeck is made of sturdy hardboard with a durable, attractive, washable vinyl covering. It folds and stores in the well behind the rear seat when not in use.

Order your Wagendeck today. Fill in the coupon below and send it along with your check or money order for 19.95.

The Wagendeck (1963) claimed to give 12 square feet of flat storage in a Beetle. Two hinge arms and brackets supplied with the kit allowed the occupants to flip the back seat forward and out of the way.

DER WUNSCH TAUSENDER VOLKSWAGEN-FAHRER NUN WIRKLICHKEIT DURCH DEN HÜLS-KOMBISITZ Pat. a.

Einbau in jeder VW-Werkstatt
Preis der Beschläge pro Sitz
24.— DM. Prospekte:
Fa. A. Hüls Kamen/Westf.

Hüls-KOMBISITZ als verstellbarer FAHRT- u. RUHESITZ

und als SCHLAF-COUCH

Some fans of vintage Volkswagens are actively seeking Hüls reclining seats, which are some of the oldest on the market. They can even convert into a bed. This beautiful ad harkens back to 1952.

Comfy Seats

VW buyers often complained about the lack of seat adjustment. Several companies already offered reclining seats in the 1950s, such as Happich (Germany) and Volkalounger (United States). Hüls also made a version as far back as 1952 that folded flat so you could comfortably spend the night with your loved one while touring.

Other similar options included products from Volmac (made in Australia) and the kit released by EMPI that could be made up into a bed. The company's 1958 catalog stated: "You'll never be caught without a place to sleep . . . and think of the hotel bills you'll save!"

As traveling the country in automobiles gained popularity after World War II, so did camping. A handful of suppliers provided tents that would fit on the Beetles' roof. Few voyagers selected travel

Dove Manufacturing made this fold-out car-top tent that could fit on Bugs, Buses, and even Ghias. Incidentally, this is a desirable pre-1960 coupe that is recognizable due to its small air vents in the nose.

Touri Camp DAS BETT AUF DEM AUTODACH

Zusammengeklappt:
SO KLEIN

Auf jedes Auto montierbar – vom VW bis zu dem
größten Reisewagen – Prospekt auf Anforderung.

Touri Camp in 2 Minuten aufgeklappt

HEINRICH ECKEL · MÜNCHEN 19

In Germany in 1957, Heinrich Eckel retailed the Touri-Camp bed/tent combination that opened in two minutes. It could also adapt to other automobiles due to its modular mounting kit.

trailers, as Volkswagens notoriously lacked power to tow them. However, one German company had a certain following: Eriba, which was the manufacturer of a compact and lightweight trailer named Puck. (Check out the end of this chapter, which features a perfect VW truck/Puck combo.)

Other companies marketed compact travel trailers. One of the most unusual was the model from Trailorboat Co. Approximately 300 have seemingly been built between 1961 and 1963. The unit had sleeping amenities for two, and the roof welcomed a small boat.

If space was an issue while traveling/camping, vacationers could purchase smaller trailers, a few of which featured a single wheel. The Allstate sold in the United States by Sears and Roebuck was a popular option in particular, having pleasing lines. Based in Nevada, O'Brien Mfg. released its own attractive version that was known as the Tag-A-Long with aerodynamically shaped taillights.

Both the Sears Allstate and the O'Brien units attached to the rear bumper and came with a single swiveling wheel. Drivers could therefore back up their cars with ease, although they had to pay

The annual Silverado VW Campout (California) caters to Volkswagen and camping buffs. Check out this nice display featuring a Trailorboat trailer. A boat fits on top of it.

Curt Kolar's 1957 Oval tows a restored 1959 Allstate trailer sold by Sears and Roebuck. He mildly customized it with deco pieces plus taillights and a license light. Note the Bug's 1950s-style crossbar hubcaps.

special attention when turning, as the fixed trailer created an overhang. But of course, VW buffs with a penchant for travels rave to this day about the campers based on the VW Type 2, such as the Westfalia specifically designed for holidays.

With vintage travel trailers and campers currently being so popular, swap meets, antique stores, and online auctions abound with travel-related items. Not all have a specific connection with the VW brand but have been embraced by VW enthusiasts. Gas-powered Coleman lanterns come to mind, in addition to Helphos spotlights. These handy pieces affix to the windshield inside the car with a suction cup. The list of period-correct camping and travel goodies seems endless, and finding some of the most elusive of the bunch can be quite addictive.

In 1967, Foreign Car Guide published this advertisement for the good-looking O'Brien single-wheel trailer. It came with a locking lid, dual taillights, and even a spare tire mounted in the back.

While not specifically intended for Volkswagens, the Helphos searchlight still has a certain following within the VW crowd. It attaches to the windshield courtesy of a suction cup.

Joe Alexander's 1963 Crew Cab and Eriba Puck Trailer

Unless you envision sleeping in the cargo bed, VW trucks may not lend themselves ideally to camping trips. Joe Alexander thereby uses his fully equipped 1963 Crew Cab to tow a small 1964 Eriba Puck trailer.

Several companies handled camper conversions during the VW Bus's Split Window era. Germany's Westfalia produced the most popular of the bunch, while the United States had models from Riviera, Sportsmobile, and more. These vehicles prove ideal for camping adventures, unlike VW trucks, although their large cargo bed certainly comes in handy to transport gear.

Joe Alexander found a solution to this conundrum: simply attaching a period-correct trailer in the back. He selected what many consider the best choice within the VW hobby: an Eriba Puck.

The Puck's size and lightweight fiberglass construction (it tips the scale around 700 pounds) makes it the ideal match for a Bus or even a Beetle. The interior is surprisingly roomy as well with six seats and one double bed, but three folks can manage to sleep comfortably. With a sink, a stove, a table, and storage space, these trailers really are perfect for short- or long-distance journeys.

Alexander's interest in VWs stems from his parents, who drove a 1962 Türkis (green) and white 11-window Bus and a 1968 Beetle. The latter was purchased new from the Kendon Motors VW dealership, hence Alexander hunted for a rare Kendon license plate frame for his Double Cab. Incidentally, many vintage dealer frames have become quite collectible. They are a great way to personalize a car, linking the latter to a specific dealership or region.

Growing up with VWs in California led Alexander to own many of them himself, starting in his teens. The South Bay, a beach area near Los Angeles where he lives to this day, offered vibrant car and surf scenes in the 1980s, and

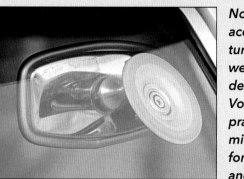

Not all vintage accessories featured in this book were specifically designed for Volkswagens. This practical German mirror was made for utility vehicles and nicely fits the theme of the Alexanders' Crew Cab.

Joe Alexander and his wife, Sally, own a great collection of air-cooled Volkswagens, mixing Beetles, Type 2s, and a Type 3 Notchback. Life is good.

Depending on the outside light, VW's L87 Pearl White can appear to be either grey or white. The Alexanders imported the Eriba Puck trailer from the UK, hence this license plate.

The ladder can stay on the truck even when in motion, as it hangs on the drip rail and bolts to the flange under the body. It gives access to a matching black roof rack.

Alexander was in the midst of it all. His love for surfing even led him to move to Hawaii for a while.

He still owns several Volkswagens today: a 1960 Westfalia camper (a right-hand drive version sold new in South Africa), an Australian 1956 Beetle with 30,000 miles, a 1962 Beetle cabriolet with 80,000 miles that has a period Judson supercharger, and a 1964 Notchback with various accessories.

A member of California's Rare Vintage Air club and Kowabunga Van Klan, Alexander enjoys cruising along the beach in his many air-cooled toys, including a Pearl White 1963 truck that he and Sally found in Florida. While looking good from far away, a closer inspection divulged an average restoration performed several years ago. The shell didn't wear its original paint anymore, so Alexander decided to have the vehicle fully redone using L87 VW Pearl White. Notice the beautiful canvas above the bed— imported from Poland.

Stark by design, Volkswagen trucks feature few frills, hence Alexander decided to individualize his ride with a handful of original vintage accessories. The most obvious are the bumper-mounted Bosch headlamps, roof rack, ladder, and the oh-so-cool Safari windows. The blades rest on a specific rubber stand when not in use.

Other obvious accessories include the Hirschmann antenna mounted next to a Hella mirror fitted with a thermometer sourced in the UK. A closer look reveals a handful of more discreet accessories, including NOS retractable VWoA front steps, which required drilling the body for installation. One of the most intriguing of the bunch

Joe Alexander had the resources necessary to refurbish the trailer's bolsters, being a professional of the bedding industry.

remains the SIMO electromagnetic rear lid latch that is activated from the cockpit and quite useful as a theft deterrent.

The interior, dressed with Wolfsburg West side panels and vinyl seat covers, welcomes a handful of accessories as well. These start with the Petri "dragon" horn button fitted to a stock-style steering wheel. Adorning the dash is a restored Bendix Sapphire II radio that keeps company with a Comfort magnetic clock.

As the Alexanders participate in a few camping-related car events every year, they went on a hunt for a small Eriba Puck trailer. Alexander said, "I found this '64 model in England. I looked abroad because they are not common here in the United States. Sure, you can find them, but they tend to be beaten up or the U.S. versions. I wanted something that was in good shape and European."

The restoration of the trailer called for changing the outside seals (a time-consuming task) and eradicating every spot of mold. Joe and Sally also searched for period accessories; thus, the trailer now features a few radios (Telefunken and Blaupunkt) and a thermometer by MotoMeter, which is a brand known for its quality car gauges.

The "kitchen" area incorporates a sink and a stove that are cleverly hidden under a counter, while a 6-volt Paluxette coffee maker helps wake up occupants in the morning. The truck and trailer combo made its first public appearance in 2019 at the Silverado VW Campout in California, where it won the "Best of Show" and "Best Campsite" awards— deservedly so.

Paluxette changed the design of its coffee machines through the 1950s and 1960s. This appears to be a later version that Alexander found in England.

Blaupunkt launched the first car radio worldwide in 1932 and has since equipped a range of vehicles, mainly from Germany. This universal unit proves perfect when picnicking; it easily slides out of its compartment.

CHAPTER 9

OLD SPEED: A TREND ROOTED IN OLD EUROPEAN AUTO RACES

For more than a century, car enthusiasts looking to personalize their vehicles with the goal of improving performance and/or appearance have found inspiration in motorsports.

The California Look mentioned in Chapter 2 is a perfect example of such an approach, as roots of the trend stem from drag racing. This type of straight-line competition remained obscure to many Europeans until the 1960s and 1970s.

On the other hand, Europe had its own tradition of motorsports, a few of which never gained real traction in America. For example, take rally racing. Practiced on various terrains (asphalt, snow, and dirt), it typically involves several timed stages by day and occasionally at night.

Arguably, the best known of the bunch is the Rallye Monte-Carlo, which has been mostly hosted in France and Monaco since 1911. Volkswagen first joined the battle in 1949 with a Beetle finishing 43rd overall and 6th in the 1500-cc class.

Belgian resident Mike Walravens used a variety of 1960s Porsche components on his 1955 Oval Window Bug, including four 356C disc brakes and steel rims. Note the homebrewed dual single-throat carb kit. (Photo Courtesy Mike Walravens)

Decades-old printed material always comes in handy when building an Old Speed project car. Hot Rod magazine published the Volkswagen Handbook in 1963. The cover shows a nicely chromed engine. (Photo Courtesy Mike Walravens)

Other Volkswagens later participated in a handful of other automobile competitions in Europe, more often than not unknown or little known in the United States. They include trials, where racers climb slippery hills; and autotest, which required drivers to quickly negotiate a low-speed course without hitting any markers.

Europeans additionally enjoyed autocross on temporary circuits that were usually set up on grass or stubble fields. (It should not be confused with the American-style of autocross, which is more akin to a slalom competition with orange cones typically used to mark a course.)

European Influences

The Old Speed trend (occasionally called Vintage Performance) has deep roots in European motorsports. To better understand its concept, picture the 1950s or 1960s living in Germany or any nearby country. You own a

In the 1950s and 1960s, Volkswagens and Porsches usually did not run hubcaps when racing. Old Speed fans often choose the same option. Fabrice Elise's 1954 sedan is fitted with 356 rims. (Photo Courtesy Mike Walravens)

Brian Conklin's 1955 Beetle seems to be ready to enter Europe's Rallye Monte-Carlo, being decked with era-correct racing goodies: Porsche 356 wheels, extra lights, leather hood straps, headlight grilles, and numbers on the doors.

The Maico front disc brake kit from the 1960s was specifically designed for the Volkswagen and Porsche 5x205-mm bolt pattern. Its compact design has the caliper located inside the disc.

Poly Pad Imports in Ohio marketed the German-made Maico's ring-type disc brake setup, which proved both lightweight and easy to install. Some folks use them to this day without any issue.

Beetle and want to improve its performance, leading to a hunt for often-elusive race-oriented parts. These parts might include engine components, a sporty steering wheel, additional instruments, and possibly a set of competition wheels. As you likely guessed, unearthing some of these goodies way back when often proved challenging due to their scarcity, the difficulty of buying them in other countries, and the lack of information pertaining to such parts.

Based on these premises, the objective of the Old Speed trend is to create a vehicle inspired by European motorsports that could have existed decades ago more often than not in the 1950s and 1960s. But here is the caveat: only vintage parts available during the set time period of your choice or perfect reproductions of these same components can be used.

To be clear, the idea isn't to deck a Volkswagen with a ton of pretty accessories with little practical use, such as a vase adorning a Bug's dash. On the other hand, the

same dash could welcome a vintage stopwatch, as rallye racers used them for decades and still use some sort of timing equipment to this day. This trend is about subdued functionality.

Completing an Old Speed project car can turn into quite an ordeal due to the difficulty of finding antique accessories characterizing this trend. Their price tags might discourage even the hardcore VW collector with the deepest pockets. Yet, finding such commodities can be rewarding, as they were often of excellent quality, having been made to last by craftsmen who took pride in their work.

Selecting a Ride

Old Speed followers often employ 1950s or 1960s Bugs for their exercise. Some enthusiasts might select a vehicle with patina, while others prefer restoring the exterior as it would have looked if it was raced during the

Many Old Speed fans find inspiration in early Porsche race cars, such as the 356 SL Gmünd that won first in class at Le Mans in 1951. It was beautifully restored in California by Emory Motorsports.

period of their choice. For example, say you are modifying a 1960 Beetle built (in your fantasy) as a race car in 1965. Most folks will choose to retain the stock VW color. Yet, others may veer toward a hue that a competitor might have picked during that same time period.

How about a tasteful Silver Metallic (paint code 5706) as seen on a 1958 Porsche Speedster for instance? After all, these sports cars have that racing edge required for an Old Speed project. You get the idea. That same school of thought applies to pretty much all aspects of the vehicle's construction.

Interestingly enough, the most hardcore Old Speed purists consider only installing items that were obtainable when the car came out of production. These assertions lead to drastic measures. For instance, a 1955 Oval Window Bug cannot receive a Judson supercharger, since it became available in 1956.

Back to the Porsche subject, the Old Speed aficionado occasionally picks components from 356s in particular, as these automobiles offer a number

This Porsche 356 could serve as inspiration for an Old Speed project car. Found in a garage, it had not been on the road since the late 1980s, when it was photographed at Emory Motorsports.

A selection of vintage performance brake systems is displayed here. Three styles of five-lug Porsche 356 drums keep company with a Maico disc brake, seen on top. (Photo Courtesy Mike Walravens)

of similarities with early Volkswagens. In fact, Porsches and Volkswagens used the same engine case until 1954. The ingenious Doctor Ferdinand Porsche was very much aware of his little flat-four's potential, so he kept on perfecting it thanks to the development of his 356 series. It could be argued that both brands started to truly drift away from each other when Porsche launched its 911, which was equipped with a 6-cylinder boxer motor, in late 1964.

Let's take a look inside Porsche's old parts bins to see what we can find. For years, 356s and Volkswagens shared the same 5x205-mm bolt pattern. However, 356s offered larger drum brakes, which can be fitted on Volkswagens with the right combination of bearings. The shoes cover about 25 percent more surface than the versions found on Beetles, thus giving additional braking power.

The 356A models had smooth drums with circumferential fins, while later 356B models (launched in late 1959) featured good-looking radial fins to improve cooling. The release of the 356C in late 1963 marked the introduction of factory disc brakes and they, too, can be fitted to Volkswagens with some modifications.

Other popular items include 356 wheels that are often installed without hubcaps. The wheels were available through dealerships or aftermarket companies back in the day. EMPI had them listed in its catalog already in 1960. Notice that most models found today measure 15 inches in diameter, but 16s were also available on Pre–A 356s produced until 1955. They have become desirable in the collectors' world.

Rich Craig located a never-run engine fitted with a genuine NOS Denzel kit that was originally assembled in 1960. Solex 32PBIC carburetors topped with Cyclone filters feed the sought-after dual-port heads.

The Denzel-equipped motor resides in Rich Craig's desirable 1952 cabriolet that is dressed with a Hella fog light and a Speedy side mirror. Sixteen-inch Porsche 356 rims hide 356A aluminum drum brakes.

Faster, Faster

Of course, installing a Porsche flat-four engine has been the dream of many VW owners—be it a 356 or 912 version. They fit with some alterations. However, be aware that these powerplants can be a costly option. Sure, they look great in an Old Speed project car, but a more powerful VW engine can be built on a tighter budget.

The most desirable conversion remains the four-cam Carrera motor, although the six-digit price tag no doubt dissuades most enthusiasts. Denny Aker's 1963 Bug seen at the beginning of Chapter 7 has been running one of these engines since the 1960s.

Unless an inexpensive 356/912 powerplant is found in good shape, modifying an era-correct VW flat-four is the best option. While the previous chapter has plenty of information about ways to hot rod a Volkswagen motor, here are a few pointers to help in your quest for vintage performance. Keep in mind that Volkswagen introduced its dual-port heads in 1967, hence Old Speed–inspired

A Porsche flat-four will fit in a Beetle with some alterations. Bond Fletcher's 1953 Split runs a 912 engine complete with a Porsche H-style oil filter canister on the fan shroud.

Vintage exhaust systems can be hard to come by, as many tend to deteriorate quickly when used. These are from (left to right): Super Sprint, EMPI, and likely Kadron. (Photo Courtesy Mike Walravens)

Need an extra gauge? How about one of these? Clockwise, from top left are the 1950s VDO for Karmann Ghias, Economotors, Koch/Okrasa, MotoMeter, Split-era VDO, and Shorrock.

Based in Germany, Riechert Tuning has been manufacturing and repairing carburetors since 1958. One of its kits with dual Solex 28PICs resides in the back of Fabrice Elise's 1954 Bug. (Photo Courtesy Mike Walravens)

cars typically use the prior single-port versions.

Back in the day, brands such as Speedwell, Okrasa, and Denzel had a certain following within VW racing circles. So, many of these suppliers' components are great candidates for an Old Speed project car. Don't forget the various superchargers available from Judson, PEPCO, M.A.G., and Shorrock for instance. Consider adding an old exhaust system from Abarth, Ansa, or EMPI as well.

So, most of them have turned to rust since the 1950s or 1960s. Accurate reproductions certainly come in handy though. Speaking of reproductions, Flat4 in Japan

offers neat mesh air filters and Fram-style oil filters very much in the spirit of the Old Speed trend.

Build cost can be kept to a minimum with some imagination. Besides the prevalent engine kits available on the market decades ago, why not consider creating a setup based around a pair of Solex 32PBI carburetors for instance? Altering manifolds and making the carburetor linkage by employing old parts found at swap meets could do the trick. Ultimately, staying true to a powerplant specific to a certain era is paramount. For example, a 2387-cc motor built around a 1975 fuel-injected Beetle case does not belong to the Old Speed category.

EMPI's 1960s Transispark ignition kit (top) consisted of an ignition box and coil. Coils (bottom) were made by Bosch in Germany, Esswein in France, and Judson in the United States. (Photo Courtesy Mike Walravens)

The Racer's Outfit

Lowering the suspension is a subject of contention. Some competition-oriented Bugs had only the rear of the car dropped decades ago to improve handling. A handful of racing Porsche 356s have apparently been lowered at all corners for the same reason starting in the second half of the 1950s. Individual tastes dictate what to do about the topic.

Mentioned earlier, Porsche 356 wheels remain a favorite within the Old Speed community, as very few other models were available until 1965/1966. Yet, models introduced around these dates, such as EMPI Sprintstars, Räders, and magnesium BRMs, fit a vehicle inspired by a late-1960s rally racer. Of course, genuine vintage rims should be preferred in lieu of reproductions, and forget about low-profile tires. High-tech products don't have their place on such project cars, as the name Old Speed entitles.

Completing the outfit might call for a pair of extra fog lights mounted on the front bumper or via one-off brackets if removing the bumper blade. Some folks like to install leather hood straps, while others prefer Porsche 356–style headlight grilles to protect the glass. The race car vibe is occasionally enhanced with painted or taped stripes over the shell plus racing numbers on the doors.

When it comes to the interior, a sport-oriented steering wheel and a few additional vintage gauges might adorn the dash to complement the stock speedometer.

Martin Kircher's 1957 sunroof Bug incorporates various race-oriented details: drilled bumpers, extra lights, headlight grilles, a center-fill gas tank (note the hole in the hood), and stickers.

Any of the antique steering wheels displayed here will look good in an Old Speed project car. They include Porsche and aftermarket models, many from EMPI. (Photo Courtesy Mike Walravens)

Keeping track of your gas tank level is essential in competition. Therefore, it is important in an Old Speed Volkswagen too. The top gauges are from Beck, Dehne, and VDO; the bottom has two examples from MotoMeter. (Photo Courtesy Mike Walravens)

Add a tachometer, an oil temperature gauge, and a fuel gauge (if your Volkswagen doesn't come with one), and you're in business. Incidentally, speaker grilles for Oval Window Beetles designed to house an aftermarket tachometer can still be found to this day.

The Later Models

The first chapter of this book mentions Economotors's EMPI GTVs (sold from 1966 until the 1970s in the United States) as well as Belgium's D'Ieteren's Mach 1 Beetles released in Belgium in 1964 with help from Okrasa in Germany. Old Speed fans occasionally find inspiration in these two models due to their sports car edge. Want to give an American twist to the former? Adding more parts from EMPI, Judson, and the like might do the trick. Want to give a European twist to the latter? Goodies from Speedwell (UK) or Kamei (Germany) could be considered.

Also, keep in mind that other VW models are worthy candidates, especially Karmann Ghias due to their sporty lines. The Type 3 offerings include a handful of aspirants, too, with the well-equipped 1500S Notchback fitting the bill in particular.

Is there a year limit to the Volkswagens that can potentially be used as a foundation for an Old Speed project? The subject is open to debate. A fringe of the vintage VW scene only considers pre-1968 models. But then again, why not accept later offerings, especially since the German manufacturer began supplying special editions with extra grunt (or at least a sporty appearance) in 1972?

Based on the just-released 1965 Beetle, D'Ieteren's special-edition Mach 1 came with additional VDO tachometer and a Koch oil temperature gauge set in a black-painted dash. (Photo Courtesy Mike Walravens)

Several neat EMPI accessories adorn Stéphane Dendievel's 1963 Ghia convertible: a GT steering wheel, radio, rev counter, and three gauges under the dash (oil pressure, oil temperature, and amps).

It isn't often that one sees Speedwell Sprint carburetor kits. The Stromberg carburetors are supported by a hefty bracket bolted to the fan shroud's back. Such a setup equips Fabian Dewar's Belgian 1961 Bug. (Photo Courtesy Mike Walravens)

Europe's 1300S and 1303 Rally (a yellow Super Beetle with matte black hood and engine lid) come to mind. By the time these two versions hit the market, companies on both sides of the Atlantic Ocean supplied popular products, such as Riechert and TDE in Germany as well as DDS and Auto-Haus in the United States.

Theo Decker Essen (TDE) was founded in Essen, Germany, in the late 1950s. TDE supplied various high-performance goodies during Volkswagen's air-cooled era. Among them was this dual-carburetor kit (1972).

A refurbished TDE 1300 carburetor kit tops the engine of Eric Malevez's 1966 sedan. Notice the vintage orange Fram oil filter that was embraced by hot rod, Volkswagen, and Porsche owners. (Photo Courtesy Mike Walravens)

Let's Hit the Road

Due to the difficulties and cost of building a proper car, the Old Speed trend remains less popular than the two other main styles: California Look and Resto Cal Look. A few enthusiasts have helped to spread the Old Speed gospel, such as Laurent Therssen, a member of the Der Autobahn Scrapers (DAS) club in Belgium. He organized the Old Speed Challenge during the DAS Drag Day in Bitburg, Germany, between 2003 and 2006.

Other events catering to the Old Speed crowd include the Petermax Müller Rennen, which is hosted every other year in Germany. Herr Müller competed with an aluminum sports car based on a shortened Beetle chassis, winning no less than 60 races in 1951. He also entered the Rallye Monte-Carlo with a Split Window Beetle.

The historic rally held in his memory caters to a select few models: up-to-1957 Beetles, up-to-1955 Buses, up-to-1959 Porsche 356s, and VW-powered coachbuilt cars. They can only be modified with period-correct components. As a result, most VW engines used there develop in the neighborhood of 50 hp with the most potent making about 80 to 90. These may seem like moderate figures, but ask any of the participants in the "Rennen," and each will confirm that competing on open roads with likeminded folks is a ton of fun.

While building an Old Speed project car remains a challenge due to the scarcity of some parts, the trend is slowly gaining traction, including in Europe. Local rules and regulations make it increasingly difficult to heavily modify vehicles, although authorities appear to be more lenient when enthusiasts use vintage aftermarket components. The latter respect the old VWs' originality, but at the same time allow their owners to personalize their rides and make them easier to use in today's hectic traffic.

The Petermax Müller Rennen welcomes a range of Old Speed Volkswagens in the vein of this group of Dutch and German Beetles. Notice how none of them feature lowered suspension. (Photo Courtesy Georg Otto)

CHAPTER 10

CALIFORNIA LOOK:
WHEN DRAG RACING MEETS THE STREET

The roots of the Old Speed trend described in the previous chapter clearly lie in well-established European motorsports that were more often than not competitions held on twisty roads as far back as the 1950s and 1960s.

On the other side of the Atlantic, some American VW enthusiasts looked elsewhere for inspiration when modifying their cars: drag racing.

While few folks knew about this sport in Europe, drag racing had become extremely popular in the United States during the same time period, thanks in part to a range of classes. Among them, the Gas categories opened to a variety of hot rods that originally prowled the streets of America. They later evolved into race-only vehicles, including a handful of stout Volkswagens.

In 2008, Rick Sadler built a Cal Look 1967 reminiscent of the Beetle he drove in the 1970s. The 2,387-cc motor delivers 227 hp. Notice the VW backup lights used as turn signals.

The California Look trend takes its inspiration in the Volkswagen Gassers that drag raced through the 1960s and 1970s. Here is a selection of them, genuine or tributes, photographed at the European Bug-In in Belgium (2008).

These are two very quick 1964 Bugs and two takes on the California Look: Dave Rhoads's green sedan has T-bars and no chrome, while John Rayburn's Volkswagen retains its bumpers and moldings.

The California Look (or Cal Look for short) mimicked these Volkswagens to a certain extent. It adopted a heavy rake with small tires in front and fat rubber in the back complemented with highly tuned engines.

The trend appeared on the boulevards of Southern California during the late 1960s and continues being influential today. However, it should be said that it has evolved for more than 50 years. Hence, if 1,000 enthusiasts were asked to describe it today, each would give a different answer. The definition of a Cal Look Volkswagen has become rather diluted over time, as some folks decided to throw custom alterations into

When creating his Cal Look project in the 1970s, Dave Rhoads adapted a custom dashboard, as was often seen at the time. VDO gauges fill the padded insert in front of the Scat steering wheel.

Dave Kanase's Volkswagen has not changed much since he finished it in the 1970s. It incorporates details typical of the time: louvers, tubular buggy bar bumpers, and tinted windows.

the mix—think chopped top and louvers, for example.

To better understand the California Look, we might need to draw a parallel with hot rodding. A hot rod from the 1940s (with wire wheels, an earth-tone paint job, and flathead V-8) looks quite different from a hot rod from the 1960s (with mag wheels, a wild-flamed paint job, and a small-block Chevy V-8). Well, the same school of thought applies to the Cal Look. This chapter puts emphasis on the early years of the trend but should also help you navigate the style through the decades and confirm that it isn't frozen in time.

Drag Strip Invasion

During the 1960s, young and cash-strapped American VW devotees looking to personalize their rides had limited choices, as the Volkswagen aftermarket industry was still in its infancy. A trip to the local auto parts store

Before the advent of the California Look, enthusiasts made do with select few wooden accessories, such as this German 1964 Pealit deep-dish steering wheel that was sold by EMPI in the United States.

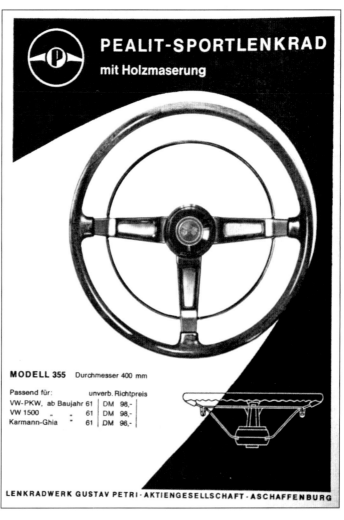

Photographed in 1969, Jim Edmiston's Volkswagen epitomizes Southern California's "Pre-Cal Look" era. The vehicle features factory moldings (but no bumpers), stock suspension height, Porsche 356 rims (front), and slotted rims sticking out of the fenders (back). (Photo Courtesy Jim Edmiston)

and a free-flowing exhaust system.

Remember that the performance-oriented enthusiast had limited wheel choices at first. Porsche 356 rims (with or without hubcaps) remained the number-one choice. Wide rear tires had a certain following with Goodyear Blue Streak rubber, for instance, often sticking out of the fenders. The rest of the outside appearance remained stock for the most part, including the original aluminum moldings, although occasionally Volkswagens can be seen with tinted rear side plexiglass windows.

The White 1963

Then along came a white 1963 sunroof Beetle that had a tremendous influence on the VW scene worldwide. When Southern California–resident Greg Aronson debuted the car in 1969, which was considered by many as the first Cal Look VW, it looked quite different from the Bugs roaming the streets.

could lead to the purchase of graphic stripes to dress the body and possibly a handful of wooden items: maybe a shift knob or a steering wheel.

As drag strips burgeoned all over the United States, these same folks began testing their Beetles over the quarter mile. They began removing excessive weight, such as the passenger seat, rear seats, and possibly the bumpers. Engines, typically displacing 1200 cc, often retained most of their factory components with perhaps the exception of a velocity stack replacing the air filter, a Bosch 010 distributor,

A most iconic hotVWs magazine cover and a most iconic Bug was the February 1975 issue that unveiled a 1963 sunroof Beetle, then owned by Jim Holmes, which paved the way of the California Look.

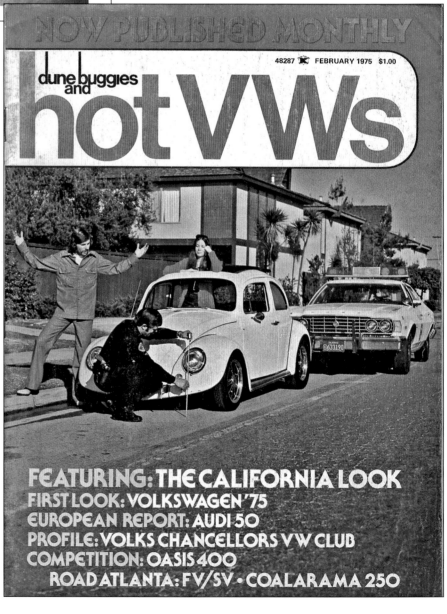

NOW PUBLISHED MONTHLY

dune buggies and

hotVWs

48287   FEBRUARY 1975 $1.00

FEATURING: THE CALIFORNIA LOOK
FIRST LOOK: VOLKSWAGEN '75
EUROPEAN REPORT: AUDI 50
PROFILE: VOLKS CHANCELLORS VW CLUB
COMPETITION: OASIS 400
ROAD ATLANTA: FV/SV • COALARAMA 250

A member of Der Kleiner Kampfwagens club, 19-year-old Mark Ramirez won America's Most Beautiful VW award at Bug-In 23 (1979), with his black 1970 sedan that was dechromed and fitted with a one-piece window kit. (Photo Courtesy Mark Ramirez)

The vehicle was covered in a non-factory bright white paint job (a Chevy truck color) and had lost all its chrome moldings on the outside for a smooth and sleek appearance. It also featured a custom dash with an array of Stewart-Warner gauges, lightweight BRM mag wheels, and the nose of the Bug sat much closer to the asphalt than any other Volkswagens at the time. Its heavy rake mimicked the drag cars of the era. Aronson relied on various engines during the late 1960s, and the most potent (tuned for drag racing) allowed the white ragtop to run in the 12-second bracket over the quarter mile.

Decades before information traveled at blistering speeds due to the internet and social media, it took years for the rest of the VW world to notice this ground-breaking Beetle. It finally received national attention in February 1975 when *hotVWs* magazine put the car on its cover with a photo by Jere Alhadeff. It showed the then-owner of the car, Jim Holmes, posing next to the vehicle and a police officer measuring the headlights' height.

This requires some explanation. During the 1970s, as the trend of lowering the front suspension became popular in Southern California, local law enforcers began giving tickets for the car being "too low" (under 24 inches from the center of the headlights to the ground).

That 1975 issue of *hotVWs* magazine was the first to mention the California Look moniker; journalist Jere Alhadeff coined the term. In addition, the same issue featured other Volkswagens that followed the trend along with a drawing by Barry "Burly" Burlile, showing the profile of a typical Cal Look Bug of the era. Not all the details shown on this artwork have stood the test of time, such as dark tinted windows and bulky nerf bars, which are rarely seen today.

The Little Tanks

Both Greg Aronson and Jim Holmes (who had bought the white 1963 in 1970) belonged to a club that greatly helped develop the California Look: Der Kleiner Panzers

Photographed after a dusty, just-for-fun pass at El Mirage Dry Lake, Fabien Bécasse's contemporary Cal Look 1967 keeps its chrome and Export bumpers. The rake and EMPI wheels have been part of the look since the 1970s.

The interior of Bécasse's car welcomes a selection of vintage EMPI goodies (steering wheel, multiple gauges, and dash pad). A Berg shifter triggers a 5-speed gearbox, while the dash plaque commemorates the first Californian Bug-In (1968).

A rare, early AutoMeter tachometer sits above the dash of Dave Mason's 1962 sedan, which is one of the fastest rides in Der Kleiner Panzers club. It runs the quarter mile in 11.48 seconds at 121 mph with a shot of nitrous oxide.

(DKP), a German name that can be loosely translated into "the Little Tanks."

Founded in 1965, DKP involved students residing in Orange County (near Los Angeles) who shared a common interest in Volkswagens. It started as a social group like many other local clubs of the time but evolved through the years as its members became interested in drag racing more often than not at Orange County International Raceway (OCIR). By the early 1970s, most club rides had morphed into beautifully detailed Cal Lookers.

DKP experienced its share of ups and downs, calling it quits in 1972, before being revived by another bunch of enthusiasts in 1975. This second generation lasted until 1979. Many had forgotten about the club until the early 1990s, when a third troupe relaunched DKP with the blessing of former members. It remains very much active to this day, organizing a variety of VW events every year.

Today's members' cars represent the California Look in all its forms and minutia. Some vehicles follow the example set by Greg Aronson decades ago. Others feature a more contemporary appearance still with a heavy rake and healthy powerplant but enhanced with stock or near-stock VW colors, factory bumpers and moldings, and an original-style interior.

Accessory Collection

During the 1970s, owners of Cal Look rides chose to remove weight wherever they could to emulate the drag cars of the era, starting with the bumpers. The police forces soon began issuing tickets for "lack of bumpers." Jim Holmes came up with a simple solution: installing four T-bars in the bumper slots. Others welded the latter shut and mounted tubular buggy bars.

Other notable accessories included sporty Talbot mirrors installed on the doors, although many other aftermarket models (Baby Tornado, Baby Turbo) became more popular during the 1980s. Some folks additionally removed the turn signals on top of the front fenders and placed round Lucas turn signals around the horn grille areas after welding their openings shut.

In 1975, the quest for an uncluttered appearance led to the removal of the doors' vent wings. This in turn resulted in the creation of the one-piece window kit in which a larger piece of glass covers each door's opening.

Plexiglas headlight covers inspired by drag Volkswagens, as seen on Dave Kanase's 1964, had a certain following during the 1970s. He chose to install genuine magnesium BRM wheels too.

To appease police officers, *Cal Look* owners have been using simple, lightweight T-bars instead of bumpers— some with a hex design. They are more subtle than the bulky nerf bars.

Lucas turn signals (often placed where the horn grilles used to reside) have been a hit with Cal Look fans for eons. Color-coded headlight rings on 1968-and-later Beetles are a neat custom touch.

Was this photo taken in Orange County, California, in 1977? No, it was at Phoenix Dragway in Germany in 2017. Ben Ooms's 1965 Volkswagen (with Porsche color and wheels) and David Baland's 1964 belong to Belgium's Der Autobahn Scrapers club.

Like many 1970s VW clubs, Der Renwagen Fuhrers had its own clubhouse that was filled with trophies. In front: a lowered and dechromed 1967 is equipped with EMPI five-spoke rims. (Photo Courtesy DRF Club)

Not all aftermarket VW wheels available had the favor of the California Look crowd, including versions that stuck out of the fenders with their tires. Steel rims from companies such as Jackman that were predominantly designed for off-road use were ruled out as well.

Not surprisingly, EMPI became a prime source for wheels, as it supplied a range of appropriate models, including magnesium BRMs and the company's own five- and eight-spoke models. Aluminum Centerlines gained in popularity during the latter part of the 1970s too.

The Porsche influence should not be underestimated, starting with 356 steel wheels and being followed by the famous Fuchs alloys that were more affordable during the second half of the 1970s. Soon, California Look fans found inspiration in certain Porsche hues and interior materials. The Cal Look trend typically called for subdued, often earth-tone colors, but the tide began to change in the 1980s, as pastels invaded everything from fashion to architecture and custom Volkswagens.

Nose-Down Attitude

To get that requisite hot rod rake, Cal Look fans first resorted to simple alterations, including the removal of leaf springs in the front suspension beam. This led to mediocre handling, but different devices welded in/on the beam later made the ride safer and more comfortable. The first devices were from Select-A-Drop and were followed by the more efficient Sway-A-Way kits.

When it comes to motors, VW owners benefited from important technical improvements, such as factory dual-port heads introduced in 1967. This made the life of engine builders easier, as they could adapt a wider range of carburetors, including the beloved Weber 48IDAs.

EMPI began experimenting with them in 1966 on its *Inch Pincher* drag car. It soon appeared in the engine compartments of countless VW quarter-milers. Cal Look VW owners followed, and the IDA remains the number-one choice within this group to this day.

Companies such as Gene Berg, Scat, CB Performance, DDS, Auto-Haus, and many others have played a key role in creating countless products for the fans of fast street cars. Crankshafts with longer strokes and big-bore cylinder/piston kits allowed enthusiasts to build 2180-cc engines during the 1970s as well.

During that same time period, Cal Look aficionados modified the interiors of their cars courtesy of sports seats and custom dashes. They frequently complemented with EMPI, VDO, or Stewart-Warner gauges and an array of switches. These folks additionally followed the

The appearance of Cal Look motors has not changed much over time, as is exemplified by Don Brown's 1967. His 2,332-cc flat-four relies on Weber 48IDA carburetors, an MSD ignition, and a Volkswagen Thing fan shroud, which was chosen because it lacks heating ducts.

Magnetos are very much part of the California Look. Being heavy, they require a sturdy bracket. Check out the neat EMPI sender adapter.

Ben Ooms's Bug painted Porsche Gold Green features an era-correct interior: Paddy Hopkirk 1960s seats, Berg shifter, VDO gauges in a dechromed dash, and a Springalex steering wheel.

upholstery trends of the era, often using black vinyl or occasionally fabric found in Porsches.

The Sleeper Edge

Through the late 1970s and especially the 1980s, the Cal Look scene witnessed some important changes. The style not only affected Beetles but also other models—most importantly Karmann Ghias and Type 3s.

An increasing number of followers adopted bright and intricate paint jobs with graphics; some even started to slightly lower the back suspension of their rides (*gasp!*).

The 1990s saw a return of a factory stock appearance (colors, bumpers, moldings, and interiors), while tons of aftermarket equipment made it easy to build reliable 2.3-liter engines capable of delivering more than 180 hp. Contemporary Cal Look cars have morphed into true sleepers, looking harmless to the untrained eye yet

becoming terrors when the driver puts the pedal to the metal. This concept continues being embraced the world over as far away as Japan and Germany.

You can bet Doctor Ferdinand Porsche, the talented brain behind the Beetle, didn't expect such remarkable developments when he created his Volkswagen before World War II.

There are no sports seats in this 1967 sedan. Instead, the owner added factory VW units. They might look stock, yet the upholstery subtly integrates a traditional Cal Look pattern from the 1970s called "fat biscuit."

Some Volkswagen enthusiasts began modifying Karmann Ghias in the 1970s, although they became more popular in the 1980s. Dustin Petrasek (DKP club) recently built this 1969 coupe on Porsche Fuchs rims.

Russ Welch's 1952 Beetle

Russ Welch's 1952 Split Window Bug is a great example of the Cal Look Volkswagens that prowled the So-Cal streets during the 1970s. He started wrenching on it in 1973.

Welch built a long-standing reputation within the VW hobby thanks to a salvage yard he owned (Russ's VW Recycling) that opened in 1983. Ten years earlier, he purchased a 1952 Beetle for $600 and set to morph it into a fast street car with 2,180-cc power.

Welch often raced it at the old Irwindale Raceway with his friends from the Valley Volks Klub (VVK). After the track closed in 1977, Welch took it apart to redo it, although the project never gained the momentum he hoped for. He still managed to gather various rare parts, such as magnesium BRM rims, an early 1950s cabriolet decklid, etc.

By 1989, the body had received a few coats of fresh paint, using Sage Green (a color typical of many VW Bay Window Buses). The chassis was converted to Super Beetle-style independent rear suspension (IRS). Then, the restoration came to a grinding halt.

Fast-forward to 2009, when friend Dave Galassi offered to resurrect the Split as a token of gratitude for hiring him back in the 1980s at Russ's VW Recycling. Sadly, Welch was diagnosed with cancer a few years later, hence Galassi got into gear to complete the car's resurrection.

The project finally hit the street in 2012, looking fantastic and equipped with a potent 2,165-cc motor. It features a long list of old-school components, such as a Gene Berg linkage, a Thunderbird exhaust system, and a DDS traction bar. Squeezing fat M&H tires proved to be a bit of a challenge, although friend George Schmidt came to the rescue and narrowed the trailing arms 2 inches per side. Wider Type 3 rear drum brakes improve stopping distances too.

Some VW fans might recognize the upholstery material used in the cockpit. It came from a Westfalia Bay Window Bus camper. Galassi purchased two Westfalia rear pads that provided enough plaid material to cover most of the components, including the side panels and the Saab Sonett seats that were originally installed by Welch in 1975. The final touch came in the shape of 40-year-old VVK stickers fitted on the side window.

Welch enjoyed his Split Window until 2015, when cancer took his life. He is still dearly missed by the VW community, but the vehicle is in good hands, as his friend Dave Galassi often drives it.

Being a pre-October 1952 model, this Split does not have any vent wings on the doors. It was also "dechromed at the factory" being a Standard version that lacked moldings at the time.

Compact Saab seats installed in 1975 look right at home in the cockpit. The upholstery mixes a few square yards of black vinyl and vintage VW Westfalia material.

Delivering 178 hp, the engine employs a range of old-school components, such as a Bosch 010 distributor, an antique Berg linkage, and a Santana pulley.

Aftermarket companies have been supplying bullet-style mirrors for decades, such as Talbot (Germany) and TEX (England) as seen here.

CHAPTER 11

RESTO CAL LOOK:
LOW AND LOADED WITH ACCESSORIES

The 1990s witnessed some important stylistic changes. Along with custom paint graphics, the pastel and loud colors so popular during the 1980s fell by the wayside. Slowly, subdued hues (often from Volkswagen's own range) returned to the scene, thus affecting the overall vibe of the project cars being built.

California Look rides were not the only ones affected by this wind of change. A different breed of air-cooled Volkswagens began to appear at Southern Californian VW shows at the time. Their looks veered from the trend of the era, with the owners putting emphasis on factory VW colors (again), a heavy dose of vintage accessories, and slammed suspensions.

One particular group called German Folks Klub (GFK) is often credited for initiating the trend. Some aspects were shared with the old-school lowrider scene. John Canales, one of the club's longtime movers and shakers, explained: "There are quite a few Hispanics in GFK, and there always has been, which explains why lowriders had an influence on our cars."

Founded in 1950, the Grand National Roadster Show (Pomona, California) welcomes a vast range of automobiles, including a few Volkswagens. The German Folks Klub displayed this highly detailed group in 2016.

Volkswagen only manufactured 696 Hebmüller convertibles. This is Richard Rivera's No. 595, which was produced in 1950 and exhibited at the VW Classic in Southern California with many other Resto Cal rides.

How many accessories can you count? Some that can be seen include decklid vent trim, license plate toppers, license plate frames, fender script, backup light, rubber bumper guards, and chrome bumper bracket covers.

The lowriders mentioned by Canales were customarily based on two- and four-door American sedans from the 1930s and 1940s. They featured dark or earth-tone colors in general, plenty of accessories, and a low-to-the-ground stance.

Born in L.A.

These VWs have traits in common with the California Look as well from the choice of wheels to some of the exterior/interior treatment. This led VW enthusiasts worldwide to adopt a name for this new craze: Resto Cal Look, which was often shortened to Resto Cal. Through the years, American VW buffs occasionally used the term Resto Custom. Let's use Resto Cal in the context of this book, since the latter caters to an international audience.

To better understand the evolution of the trend, we need to travel back to 1982, when a group of

Ronny Garcia's sunroof 1963 Beetle features a sun visor (from Australia), which is an accessory popular with the old-school lowrider scene as well. In fact, Resto Cal Volkswagens have numerous traits in common with lowriders.

Photographed shortly after the turn of the century, these are some of the Bugs from the German Folks Klub (GFK). All are pre-1968 models, as you might expect. Mike Navarro's purple 1962 was built in 1992, hence its color.

Type 3s belong to the Resto Cal family too. Washington state's Mark Souza found a 1965 1500S and installed different add-ons, such as headlight grilles, fog lights, door-handle guards, a roof rack, and more.

The treatment of lowered suspension, vintage polished wheels, and accessories applies to VW Buses and trucks as well, as is demonstrated by Chip Hascher's 1963 Crew Cab from Ohio. It runs a 1,915-cc motor.

Roof racks have been a hit with Volkswagen owners since the 1940s and went on to equip a range of VW models, Type 2s included. They prove handy to transport coolers, luggage, and the occasional surfboard.

young lads living in a Los Angeles suburb established the German Folks Klub. The troop welcomed an eclectic assortment of air-cooled Volkswagens at first. It stayed active until 1986, when the club died due in part to the surge of the mini-truck era. Some members even built their own pickup trucks.

Two years later, GFK sprung back in action due to the efforts of several high school friends. Most members lived in Southern California at the time, but the club began to expand in the 1990s with chapters in Arizona, Texas, and Japan. A few more affiliates living in Nevada

and the United Kingdom joined the field after the turn of the century.

As the style emphasizes the cars' vintage appearance and antique accessories, only pre-1968 Beetles (with thin blade bumpers) are deemed acceptable by the group to this day. Other older VW models belong to the family as well: Split Window Buses, pre-1970 Karmann Ghias, and pre-1970 Type 3s. Although you occasionally (but rarely) see Super Beetles adopting California Look characteristics, these late-model Bugs have never been deemed acceptable by the Resto Cal community.

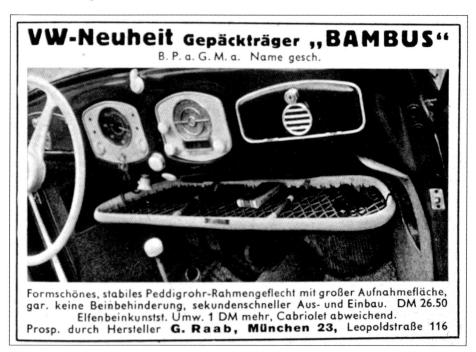

Countless companies produced goodies for the Beetles' interiors in the vein of the Bambus shelf that was popular with the Resto Cal fans. Check out the desirable glove-box doors.

loses between 3 and 5 inches. In the back, reindexing the factory spring plates (usually one or two notches) or using adjustable plates drops the vehicles to a level deemed acceptable.

Vintage-style wheels have always been associated with the Resto Cal trend, with five-spoke EMPIs (often replicas), BRMs, and Porsche 911 Fuchs being popular during the 1990s. Today, the same Fuchs rims have a huge following due to several high-quality reproduction models being available.

Favorite sizes include 15x4.5 for the front (as they offer a deep offset) with early-style 15x6 in the back. They need to shine—hence the decision of having them either fully polished or chromed. Narrow radial tires measuring 135-15 or even 125-15 equip the front, and they are often complemented with 205/65-15s in the rear.

How Low Can You Go?

By the mid-1990s, Volkswagens belonging to the club abided by certain specifics—all very much prevalent today. The stance remains a key element of the look with suspension always being lowered front and back without the use of any airbag kit. Installing a narrowed front beam is one trick to get the nose of the cars even closer to the asphalt without rubbing the fender lips. It typically

While not as prevalent as during the 1990s, fully polished EMPI five-spoke wheels (original as seen here or reproductions) remain very much part of the look. The original version has a two-piece construction.

This is the typical Resto Cal stance that is seen on Steve Raaff's 1957 sedan. Raaff has a narrowed/adjustable front axle beam, lowered rear suspension, no airbag suspension, early Porsche 911 wheels (15x4.5 and 15x6), and 135-15 and 205/65-15 tires.

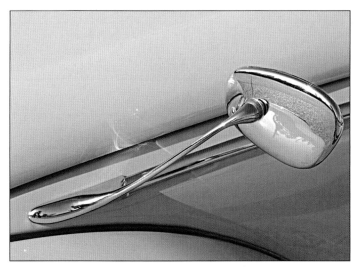

Albert offered a range of aftermarket VW mirrors, including a model that clipped on a Bug's window frame. Yet, the company is often associated with its swan neck model that is mounted above the Beetle's fenders.

To this day, you can find old accessories for Oval Window dashboards fairly easily (as exemplified by this 1955 model). It has the following equipment: a VDO clock, a "Big M" Motorola radio, a glove-box door pull, and a VW steering column lock. The vintage coin holder affixes to the windshield with a suction cup.

From Reproduction to Genuine

Back in the early days of the Resto Cal trend, enthusiasts frequently selected reproduction accessories mostly due to their reasonable cost. Among them were fender guards, fog lights, and roof racks, although the latter has lost some of the following in recent times. Soon, owners of these cars started to look for the more elusive original pieces. The hunt was on for genuine vintage accessories.

The list of goodies used on the vehicles' exterior includes additional Hella front light and rear backup lights, mirrors (occasionally combined with a spotlight), Hirschmann red-tip antennas, dealer license plate frames, and the ubiquitous pop-out windows. A handful of folks like to install Foxcraft fender skirts that tend to enhance the super-low stance as well as flagpoles that attach to the front fender lips.

Considering the astounding number of accessories available for the interior, the cockpit of these same cars oozes with rare pieces. They might include a Petri steering wheel, MotoMeter gauges, a clock, a German or American radio, a trick rearview mirror, a Hurst shifter, reclining seats, and much more.

During the previous century, fans of the style often used 1958 to 1967 Beetles for their exercise. However, enthusiasts now search for more desirable VW models, such as pre-1958 Bugs (Split and Oval Windows), Hebmüllers, pre-1960 Karmann Ghias, and 1950s Buses.

The overall quality of the rides selected has improved steadily over the decades with pan-off restorations becoming the norm. Then again, we are not in 1982 anymore, when a 1967 Volkswagen was 15 years old and therefore still likely in good shape!

Fender skirts tend to visually lower a slammed Volkswagen, as Frank Casares's 1958 sunroof Beetle shows. The car is painted Yukon Yellow, which is a popular air-cooled Volkswagen color.

This angle of Christian Schilling's 1956 ragtop from Virginia clearly shows the result of narrowing the front axle beam. The 15x4.5 Porsche Fuchs wheels are deeply set under the fenders.

The cockpit of Christian Schilling's Volkswagen features the following add-ons: VDO gauges, a glove-box door tab, a large red emergency lights knob of unknown origin, a dash handle, Bambus tray, and locking steering column.

Although rare aftermarket accessories are welcome, Resto Cal VW owners also seek ancient pieces sold by VW dealers, such as this locking shifter. The additional ashtray is a neat touch.

More Displacement

The trend revolves around the idea of driving low and slow rather than racing between traffic lights. Therefore, engines are often stock or mild. This statement proves especially true through the 1980s and 1990s, when young owners of Resto Cal Volkswagens had limited budgets. Yet slowly, the same crowd began installing more powerful engines ranging from 1.9 to 2.3 liters that were usually fed via dual Weber carburetors.

The GFK remains one of the main representatives of the style to this day. Their cars are reaching new levels now. The team displays up to 20 vehicles at major So-Cal events, such as the massive El Prado Show & Shine as well as the world-famous Pomona Swap Meet that is held seven times a year. You can't miss their rides, as they all feature a painted rear window with the German Folks logo that has been part of GFK's requisite outfit since 1994.

The group's efforts have inspired other enthusiasts to follow in their footsteps all over the world. A club based in Brazil aptly called Brazilian Folks comes to mind. Their Volkswagens adopt the GFK's guideline, although members use not only models we all know (Bugs, Buses etc.) but also local production (Brasilias, four-door 1600s etc.). From L.A. and Rio de Janeiro to Tokyo and London, the Resto Cal trend will no doubt continue enticing Volkswagen buffs for years to come due to its good taste, plenty of attitude, and an impressive range of accessories.

Seen at the Grand National Roadster Show is the late Carlos Guzman's amazing 1957 Microbus. It is one of the most desirable models, being a 23-window version and painted VW Sealing Wax Red and Chestnut Brown.

You can expect the German Folks Klub to show up en masse at popular VW meets, including the massive El Prado Show & Shine in California. Members drive accessory-laden cars complemented with a painted rear window.

Being stark by design, Standard Beetles might look awkward with too many add-ons, at least to the Resto Cal crowd. Darren Dilley of British Columbia, Canada, exercised restraint with his low-mileage 1951 sedan—but what a great stance!

Based in Arizona, Buddy Hale did a fantastic job restoring Brian Ortiz's 1961 23-window Type 2. Power for this "Best of Show" winner comes from a 2,276-cc motor with dual Weber carburetors.

Victor Gonzalez's 1951 Beetle

Victor Gonzalez has owned close to 30 air-cooled Volkswagens through the years. But like many enthusiasts, he dreamed of owning a Split Window Beetle, and then along came this rough and incomplete 1951 sunroof model.

Since the turn of the century, Gonzalez, a German Folks Klub member, had the good fortune of finding some great vintage Volkswagens, including a few that he morphed into high-quality project cars. The most recent was a road-scraping 1965 Type 3 Notchback. But in the back of his mind, he still longed for an early-1950s Bug. His quest finally turned into reality when a friend turned him on to a 1951 model with a factory ragtop.

The car, or rather the rolling shell, had been for sale for quite some time. However, no one pulled the trigger due to its rough shape and missing hard-to-find components. The fact that the vehicle still had its original fenders, hood, and doors convinced him to put his pile of dollars to good use. Most VW enthusiasts would have been intimidated by the prospect of reviving such a survivor—but not Gonzalez. He happens to love parts hunting.

Ryan Osborn at ELR VW Preservation handled the bulk of the restoration, using several components shipped from Finland by Mika Virtanen, who is the man behind Restoration Panels. The list included the front firewall, window channels, and heater channels.

Gonzalez then purchased a few gallons of L73 VW Chestnut Brown paint, a color that is correct for 1951 Bugs, and had it applied by Vintage Bodywerks. Yet, a visit to a local Volkswagen event made him reconsider his choice, as he noticed other Splits painted the same hue. He thereby thought outside the box and selected a vintage Bus color: L312 Palm Green. It proved to be a great match to the Chestnut Brown paint, so he used it to dress the engine tin, fuel tank, and a few other components.

Gonzalez handled the chassis work in parallel, using new KlassicFab pan halves and semi-gloss powder coated black paint. Several GFK members came to the rescue with a handful of parts, including a 4-inch narrowed front beam and a set of genuine vintage 15x4.5 and 15x6 Porsche 911 Fuchs rims. They cover four Wilwood disc brakes. Note the very narrow Firestone 125R15 and fatter 215/65R15s tires.

The use of CB dropped spindles and adjustable 3-inch dropped spring plates from Gilbert Banuelos ensure a decent ride. Power comes from a 110-hp 1,915-cc engine fed by pair of Weber 44IDF carburetors.

The hunt for rare parts led Gonzalez to sellers located all over the United States and faraway countries. During a trip to the UK, he scored an accessory side mirror; he then added a VW hood emblem from Kaefer Nostalgie along with various NOS or restored chrome pieces, such as bumpers and guards uncovered in Pennsylvania.

Great finds included an über-cool mirror/Kienzle clock unit, smooth pop-out windows, and ribbed semaphores. Other desirable goodies sourced worldwide dress the cockpit, starting with the glove-box doors (Germany), ashtray and window winders (Argentina), Telefunken radio (Oklahoma), front seats (Kansas), etc. Bob Koch supplied the Standard Beetle steering wheel and the glass with correct Sekurit logos.

Time to trim the interior. Gonzalez knocked at the door of one of the most prominent VW upholstery shops in California: West Coast Classics Restoration (WCCR). The team led by Lenny Copp handled the seat covers and side panels, using Braun material correct for Split Windows. The same cloth resides inside the glove boxes.

Restoring the Split was certainly not a project for the faint of heart. Gonzalez said, "It seemed like everything went wrong at one point or another. I thought I'd never see the end of this project."

The old Volkswagen turned out terrific in the end. In fact, it perfectly represents the quality you can expect from German Folks Klub cars.

Now, that's low! Like many of his GFK friends, Gonzalez runs no shocks in the front and simply relies on the beam's narrowed torsion leaves. Among the car's rare parts was early, smooth pop-out windows.

Early Beetles could be equipped with an antenna that was typically fitted in front of the windshield. The upper mount sat on top of a dimple that was stamped by the VW factory in the roof's front area.

The dash houses sought-after glove-box doors with grilles mimicking the ones found in the front fenders (horn grilles). Restoration guru Bob Koch supplied the three-spoke steering wheel.

Period accessory buffs will no doubt appreciate the Kienzle clock. It attaches to the stem of the day/night mirror, which is another uncommon piece.

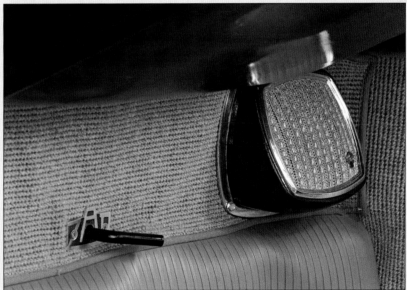

A vintage Blaupunkt speaker box hides a modern tweeter that is connected to the Blaupunkt radio. In case you wondered, the black lever (left) opens and closes the gas tank's reserve tab on pre-1962 Bugs.

CHAPTER 12

A NOTCH ABOVE:
DETAILED, STYLISH, AND FULLY ACCESSORIZED

To conclude this book, how about a study of five cars that have truly wowed the crowd in recent years due to their level of detailing and selection of rare accessories? Choosing the vehicles to illustrate this chapter was challenging, considering the craftsmanship displayed by many of today's VW project cars.

The final selection includes a trio of Oval Window Volkswagens from Southern California, a 1966 Beetle from Germany, and a 1957 cabriolet from Washington state. Get ready for some accessory overload!

There is a certain theme between these three Bugs that are all Oval Window models, although there are also subtle differences. The German Folks Klub trio uses genuine, early Porsche 911 Fuchs wheels that are fully polished. They measure 15x4.5 and 15x6.

From left to right are Jose Piña, Tony Chavez, and Vince Rodriguez. On Piña's red 1956, notice the simple European front bumper fitted with accessory rubber strips over the guards and an EMPI bumper bar that was meant to protect the blade.

Jose Piña's Red 1956

The three Oval Window Volkswagens that open this chapter all belong to the German Folks Klub (GFK). After owning a 1964 Bug and a 1966 Bus, Piña longed for a pre-1958 Beetle (either a Split or Oval Window) like many VW enthusiasts. He ultimately found an excellent candidate thanks to one of his club friends based in Arizona. Though looking rather sad, the bone-stock, U.S.-specs 1956 vehicle in question showed no rust, which is a rather unusual find today.

Piña entrusted talented craftsman Paul Smoot (a name often associated with GFK) to take care of repairing, prepping, and painting the shell. The exterior features hard-to-find components, such as the 1950s Bosch headlight lenses and European semaphores along with collectible accessories. The Hella spotlight comes to mind.

Other rarities found their way into the cockpit, including a restored VW steering wheel with a Petri horn ring and St. Christopher horn button. Power comes from a healthy 2,109-cc (94x76-mm) motor with Weber 48IDA carburetors.

Was this the factory color? No, but it could have been. Piña selected to have the paint specially blended for his 1956 sedan featuring European semaphores.

Based in Germany, Hella made a number of automotive lighting products highly regarded within the Volkswagen scene. They included this rare example that doubles as a mirror.

Among the beautiful accessories is a VDO clock set in a bespoke speaker grille in addition to a German Blaupunkt radio complemented with a shortwave adapter. The Blaupunkt badge on the ashtray is a neat touch.

Piña pushed the details as far as having the Blaupunkt radio casing entirely chromed. In front of it resides a highly desirable SWF window washer bottle. Don't expect Jose to set a luggage piece in this trunk.

Ahead of the Gene Berg shifter, a single original Blaupunkt speaker supplies the tunes. It fits under the dash on the front cross panel.

Tony Chavez's Black 1955

Growing up in and around Los Angeles, California, during the 1980s could be quite adventurous. Some neighborhoods were riddled with violence as Tony Chavez will confirm. He was stabbed in the chest when a robber tried to get his 1960 Beetle. While he lived to tell the tale, the experience soured him from owning a Volkswagen ever again. But a surprise encounter in a parking lot with several friends and their Volkswagens years later made him contemplate getting one again.

He therefore sold his collection of 1,000 Hot Wheels Redlines toys from the 1970s to fund the purchase of a vehicle, settling on a 1955 owned by Bob and Teresa Koch. The two notorious personalities in the U.S. VW scene run a VW restoration shop called Koch's. With the car fully redone by the company and Chavez, the body received various accessories.

Being a U.S.-specifications 1955 model, the black Bug retains its bullet turn signals and towel-rail bumpers. Koch's, which is a So-Cal Volkswagen restoration shop, did a fantastic job with the straight-as-an-arrow paint job, using a House of Kolor mix.

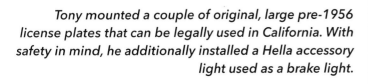

Tony mounted a couple of original, large pre-1956 license plates that can be legally used in California. With safety in mind, he additionally installed a Hella accessory light used as a brake light.

How many add-ons do you count? There is a Porsche 356A steering wheel and horn ring, a Golden Lady horn button, an SWF red-tip turn signal switch, a VDO trip speedometer, Perohaus clock, Blaupunkt radio with shortwave adapter, VW glove-box door pull, and more.

One accessory was the VW of America passenger-side mirror. This dealer-supplied piece allows the driver to look behind through the windscreen rather than the door. The interior welcomes its share of add-ons too: a Hurst shifter, a SWF rearview mirror with light, a VW-logoed glove-box door pull, etc. Under the decklid lurks a Weber 48IDA-fed 1,915-cc (94x69-mm) engine built by Koch's.

Vince Rodriguez's Ultramaroon 1955

SWF made this very cool mirror topped with a switch that turns on a courtesy light. How often do you see these?

With a packed garage, Vince Rodriguez didn't need an extra project car, especially since he wanted to concentrate on an ambitious restoration based on a right-hand-drive 1955 Oval Window Bug. Yet, he could not pass the opportunity to purchase another 1955 found in a local body shop. He originally planned to resell the car, but he decided to keep it, being in much better condition than his other classic Beetle.

In typical German Folks Klub fashion, the L276 VW Ultramaroon 1955 sedan uses a narrowed axle beam to tuck the front wheels under the fenders. This one has lost no less than 6 inches.

Numerous after-market hood badges have been available through the years. Rodriguez isn't certain of this version's origin. It shows the city of Wolfsburg's crest in bright red.

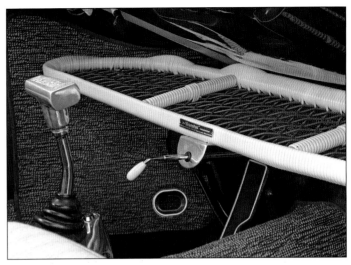

In front of the Gene Berg locking shifter, Vince mounted a "Ra-Bambus Kleingepäckträger" (small luggage rack) manufactured in Munich, Germany. It supports the fuel tap extension.

Putting the sedan back in shape thereby proved fairly straightforward. He applied a few coats of L276 Ultramaroon paint (yet slightly modified) used by Volkswagen during the 1950s. A selection of accessories was added, including the popular pop-out side windows that complement the exterior, while more goodies add some flair to the interior (a "Big M" Motorola radio, a VDO trip speedometer, a VDO clock, and a Petri steering wheel).

As the vehicle now runs a potent 2,221-cc (94x80-mm) motor with dual Weber carburetors, Rodriguez elected to install four Wilwood disc brakes. His finished project car now belongs to the pack of German Folks Klub Ovals, the most popular VW model within the group.

Jan Goeman's Sea Sand 1966

As might be expected, plenty of vintage VW accessories can still be found in Germany, which is Jan Goeman's home country. His quest led him to fit more than 100 of them on his 1966 sedan that he restored himself. One of the most unusual parts is the front axle beam that was modified in the 1960s by racer/tuner Ewald Stock, who lowered it by using Porsche 356 components. Goeman additionally selected a set of rarely seen Rostyle wheels (South African Sprintstars).

VW fans will quickly notice several popular add-ons, such as the WEGU mud flaps. However, others may not be as easy to spot: Jokon aftermarket front turn signals, a two-point Ruby antenna, genuine VW hinge covers, and more.

The same statement applies to the interior, ranging from a Koch Oettinger oil temperature gauge (in a MotoMeter steering column bracket) to a Herco Fixogas

The vehicle uses two round mirrors that are correct for the 1955 model year. It also has a Hirschmann red-tip antenna, which is a brand popular with both Porsche and Volkswagen owners.

There are more than 100 add-ons sprinkling Jan Goeman's 1966 sedan. The front bumper carries a Miller fog lamp and an additional high-power Bosch horn, while a Nordland visor from the 1950s provides shade to the driver.

The restored single-wheel Löfa trailer, which was found rotting in a Swedish forest, is a great conversation piece. Accessories range from large (original 1950s Aviation roof rack) to small (HUMA red-tip flagpole on the front fender).

mechanical cruise control hidden behind the pedals. Not surprisingly, the vehicle carries quite a bit of extra weight, so Goeman installed a 1,641-cc (87x69-mm) engine topped with dual 40-mm Kadron carburetors for some needed punch.

Jokon began manufacturing automotive equipment in 1948 and specialized in lighting. Among its products designed for Beetles is this license plate light that also incorporates backup lights.

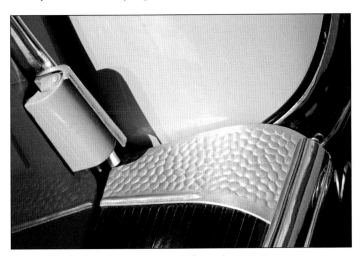

Most of these rare items came from large vintage car swap meets, such as the famous Veterama in the city of Mannheim, Germany. Check out the Stahlgruber running board aluminum trim.

Rubber bumper guard covers came in different shapes, although you rarely see this version manufactured by WEGU in Germany. The red Hella light is more common.

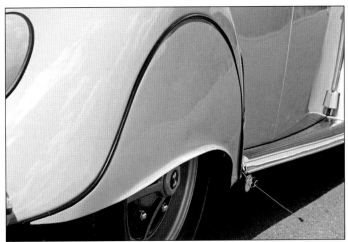

Goeman found a pair of Foxcraft fender skirts, but they proved beyond repair. Being an industrial mechanic and talented metalworker, he had the skills to fabricate exact duplicates.

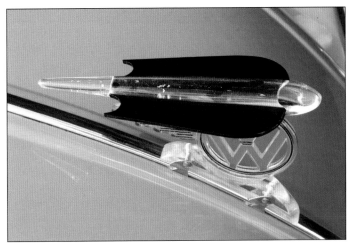

Hood ornaments often produced in brass, zinc, or bronze with a chrome-plated finish have been part of automotive history since the early 20th century. This Australian Acrylglas decoration was made of acrylic.

Window vent shades, Perohaus rain gutter trim, a parking light, and a passing eye dual mirror allowed the driver to look ahead while passing vehicles on the road. Occasionally, this accessory can be seen on lowrider cars too.

When entering car shows, Goeman displays a variety of vintage goodies, such as 45 rpm records. On the passenger's door rests a 1960s Paluxette-style coffeemaker. A Helphos search light is affixed to the windshield with a suction cup.

An SWF turn signal/high beam switch complements the 1950s Petri Banjo steering wheel. Below left, a VDO tachometer graduated to 8,000 rpm is shown. Tunes come from a Philips radio.

Not all the add-ons found in the cockpit were specifically designed for Volkswagens. For example, take the Philips Automignon vinyl player that is attached to the parcel shelf next to a thermometer.

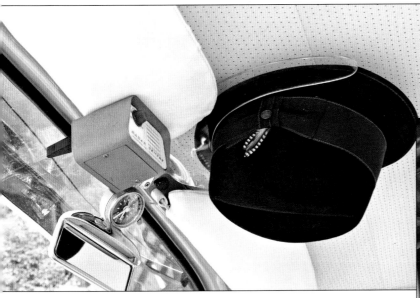

More fine add-on pieces are shown in the shape of an illuminated SWF rearview mirror (note the VDO clock), a 1963 radar Sentry Speedtrap sensor, and a Kamei hat holder with a period German hat of course.

Alan Meier's Isis Blue 1957

Even the most hardcore VW enthusiasts might have given up the restoration of Alan Meier's convertible. In fact, the bodywork started by cutting the corroded shell in two, before spending hundreds of hours on its resurrection. It ultimately received a factory 1957 cabriolet color, L232 Isis Blue, with extra metallic to brighten the mix. More shine comes courtesy of a staggering number of chromed parts, the more obvious being the Fumagalli wheels.

The topless Beetle mixes traits of both the Old Speed and Resto Cal trends. Various parts came from Australia, including the body side trim, headlight grilles, Volmac folding shifter, and seat recliners.

Meier elected to use a 36-hp engine case, which received a mixture of period-correct high-performance components, including an original Okrasa heads/dual carburetor kit (see Chapter 6). Anywhere you look, this car is a true showstopper.

Even the shifter isn't your usual unit. It folds down and has an ashtray and a locking base. In front of it resides a basket to carry small items.

Dressed with Australian side trim kit, Alan Meier's sought-after 1957 cabriolet now sits on chromed Fumagalli rims imported from Brazil. Above the bumper, rare Hella dual fog lights clamp to the hood handle.

Based in Australia, Pearlcraft handled the pearl finish on the Split Window steering wheel with chromed spokes, while North Hollywood Speedometer restored the trip-meter speedometer. A MotoMeter gauge holder affixes to the chromed steering column.

WCCR (California) did a terrific job replicating the early-style upholstery. A trio of restored MotoMeter gauges fit inside a chromed panel from the same company.

The passenger faces a compass and a locking glove-box door adorned with an original Heuer stopwatch that is one of the most collectible items on Meier's Bug.

Meier located the door-handle shields (now fully polished) in Brazil. A pocket in the door panel is ideal to carry maps and old literature, such as a 1950s Foreign Car Guide and A New Guide to Rallying.

Pedalwerks did a wonderful job with the pedal assembly. It is fully chromed and sports an older reproduction Okrasa throttle pedal. A small pedal (left) covers the dimmer switch that activates the high beam.

The finish of this trunk area is second to none. The lack of a spare wheel shows several chromed components, such as the car jack. The classic SWF bottle feeds fluid to the windshield washer jets.

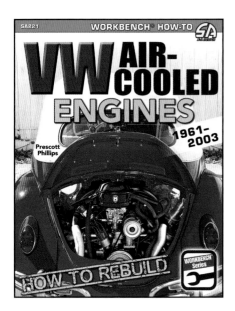

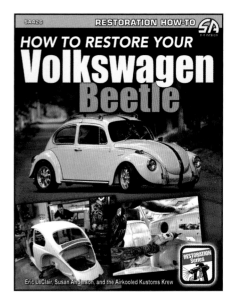
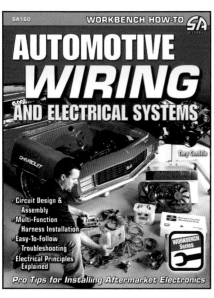